Southern Cooking Bible

Publications International, Ltd.

Copyright © 2012 Publications International, Ltd.
All rights reserved. This publication may not be reproduced or quoted in whole or in part by any means whatsoever without written permission from:

Louis Weber, CEO
Publications International, Ltd.
7373 North Cicero Avenue
Lincolnwood, IL 60712

Permission is never granted for commercial purposes.

All recipes and photographs that contain specific brand names are copyrighted by those companies and/or associations, unless otherwise specified. All photographs *except* those on pages 41, 47 and 177 copyright © Publications International, Ltd.

Campbell's® and Pace® registered trademarks of CSC Brands LP. All rights reserved.

Pepperidge Farm® registered trademark of Pepperidge Farm, Incorporated. All rights reserved.

Some of the products listed in this publication may be in limited distribution.

Pictured on the front cover: Spicy Buttermilk Oven-Fried Chicken *(page 64).*

Pictured on the back cover *(left to right):* Fresh Berry-Berry Cobbler *(page 156)* and Cheese-Topped Ham Biscuits *(page 24).*

ISBN-13: 978-1-4508-5370-5
ISBN-10: 1-4508-5370-6

Library of Congress Control Number: 2012934817

Manufactured in China.

8 7 6 5 4 3 2 1

Microwave Cooking: Microwave ovens vary in wattage. Use the cooking times as guidelines and check for doneness before adding more time.

Preparation/Cooking Times: Preparation times are based on the approximate amount of time required to assemble the recipe before cooking, baking, chilling or serving. These times include preparation steps such as measuring, chopping and mixing. The fact that some preparations and cooking can be done simultaneously is taken into account. Preparation of optional ingredients and serving suggestions is not included.

Publications International, Ltd.

Shindig Starters 4

Homestyle Breads. .24

Soups 'n Gumbos .44

Hearty Meat Dishes 64

Fish 'n Seafood 84

Sides 'n Salads 104

Cakes 'n Pies 124

Mama's Desserts 144

Classic Condiments 164

Acknowledgments 186

Index 187

Shindig Starters

brandy-soaked scallops

Makes 8 servings

1 pound bacon, cut in half crosswise
2 pounds small sea scallops
½ cup brandy
⅓ cup olive oil
2 tablespoons chopped fresh parsley
1 clove garlic, minced
½ teaspoon onion powder
Salt and black pepper

1. Wrap one piece bacon around each scallop; secure with toothpick, if necessary. Place wrapped scallops in 13×9-inch baking dish.

2. Combine brandy, oil, parsley, garlic, onion powder, salt and pepper in small bowl; mix well. Pour mixture over scallops; cover and marinate in refrigerator at least 4 hours.

3. Preheat broiler. Remove scallops from marinade; discard marinade. Arrange scallops on rack of broiler pan. Broil 4 inches from heat 7 to 10 minutes or until bacon is browned. Turn; broil 5 minutes more or until scallops are opaque. Remove toothpicks before serving.

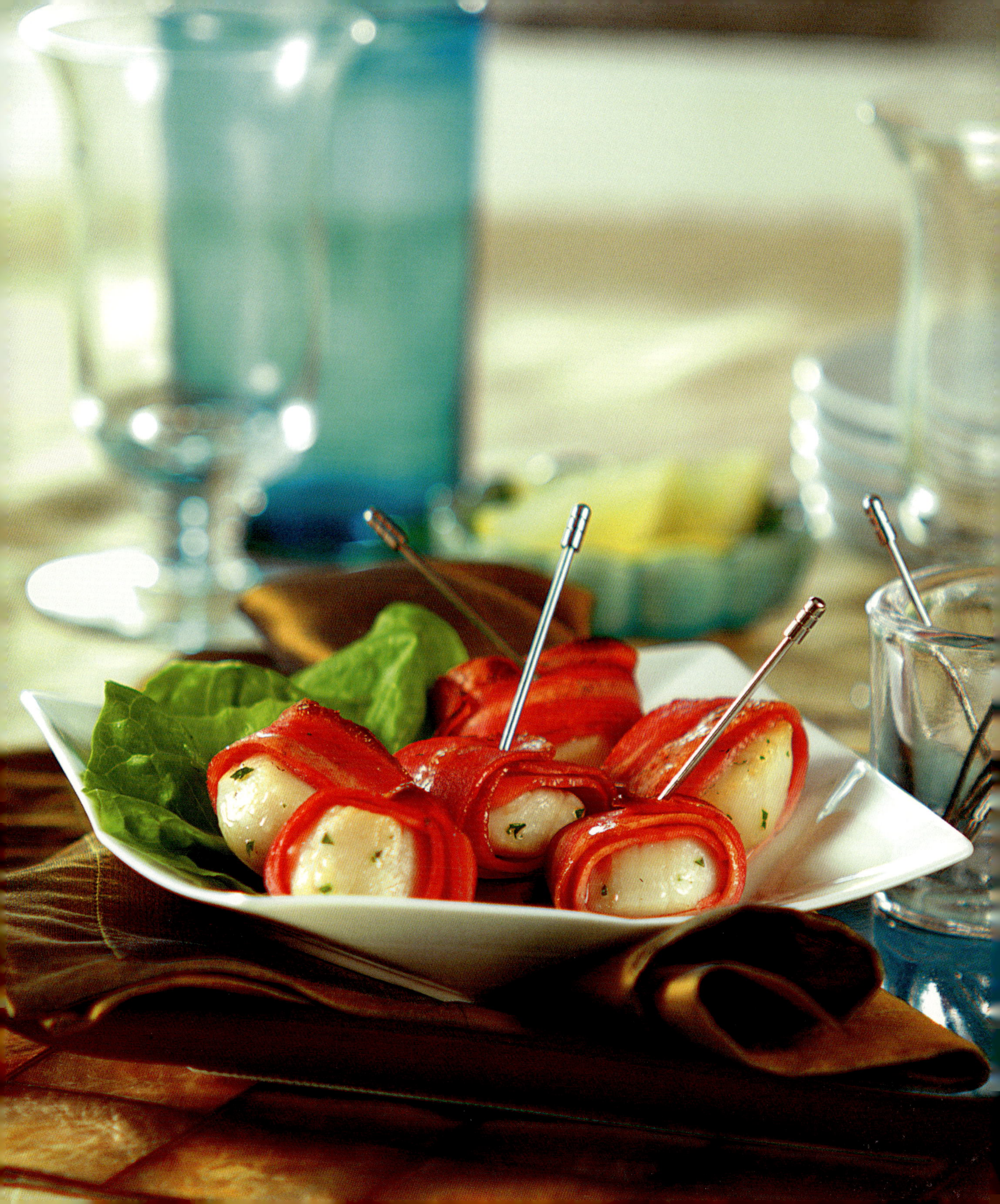

corn fritters

Makes 4 servings (8 to 9 fritters)

2 large ears corn*
2 eggs, separated
¼ cup all-purpose flour
1 tablespoon sugar
1 tablespoon butter, melted
Salt and black pepper
⅛ teaspoon cream of tartar
1 to 2 tablespoons vegetable oil

*The fresher the corn, the better the fritters.

1. Husk corn. Cut kernels from ears (1½ to 2 cups); place in medium bowl. Hold cobs over bowl, scraping with back of knife to extract juice. Transfer about half of kernels to food processor or blender; process 2 to 3 seconds or until coarsely chopped. Add to whole kernels.

2. Whisk egg yolks, flour, sugar, butter, salt and pepper in large bowl. Stir in corn mixture.

3. Beat egg whites and cream of tartar in separate large bowl with electric mixer at high speed until stiff peaks form. Fold egg whites into corn mixture.

4. Heat 1 tablespoon oil in large nonstick skillet over medium-high heat. Drop ¼ cupfuls of batter into skillet 1-inch apart. Cook 3 to 5 minutes per side or until lightly browned. Repeat with remaining batter, adding more oil, if necessary. Serve immediately.

7 - SHINDIG STARTERS

corn fritters

hot pepper cranberry jelly appetizer

Makes 16 servings

½ cup whole berry cranberry sauce
¼ cup apricot fruit spread
1 teaspoon sugar
1 teaspoon cider vinegar
½ teaspoon red pepper flakes
½ teaspoon grated fresh ginger
Assorted crackers
Sliced cheeses

1. Cook cranberry sauce, fruit spread, sugar, vinegar and red pepper flakes in small saucepan over medium heat until sugar is dissolved. *Do not boil.* Transfer to bowl; cool completely. Stir in ginger.

2. To serve, top crackers with cheese slices and spoonful of cranberry mixture.

hot crab-cheddar spread

Makes 8 to 10 servings

1 (8-ounce) container crabmeat, drained and shredded
8 ounces CABOT® Mild or Sharp Cheddar, grated (about 2 cups)
½ cup mayonnaise
¼ teaspoon Worcestershire sauce

1. Preheat oven to 350°F.

2. In medium bowl, mix together all ingredients thoroughly. Transfer to small (1-quart) baking dish. Bake for 25 to 35 minutes, or until lightly browned on top and bubbling at edges. Serve with crackers or bread toasts.

hot pepper cranberry jelly appetizer

cheddar-beer hush puppies

Makes about 36 hush puppies

    Vegetable oil for frying
1½ cups medium grain cornmeal
1 cup all-purpose flour
2 tablespoons sugar
1 teaspoon baking powder
1 teaspoon baking soda
    Salt and black pepper
1 bottle (12 ounces) lager beer
1 egg, beaten
¾ cup (3 ounces) shredded Cheddar cheese
2 jalapeño peppers,* seeded and minced

*Jalapeño peppers can sting and irritate the skin, so wear rubber gloves when handling peppers and do not touch your eyes.

1. Fill large saucepan with 3 inches of oil and heat over medium-high heat to 350°F. Line baking sheet with paper towels.

2. Combine cornmeal, flour, sugar, baking powder, baking soda, salt and black pepper in large bowl. Whisk beer and egg until combined in medium bowl. Gradually whisk beer mixture into cornmeal mixture until smooth. Stir in cheese and jalapeños.

3. Working in batches, drop heaping tablespoonfuls of batter into oil. Fry 2 minutes or until golden brown, turning occasionally. Transfer to prepared baking sheet to drain. Serve immediately.

11 - Shindig Starters

cheddar-beer hush puppies

shrimp toast

Makes 12 servings

12 large raw shrimp, peeled and deveined, tails intact
1 egg
2 tablespoons plus 1½ teaspoons cornstarch
Salt and black pepper
3 slices white sandwich bread, each cut into 4 triangles
1 hard-cooked egg yolk, cut into ½-inch pieces
1 slice (1 ounce) cooked ham, cut into ½-inch pieces
1 green onion, finely chopped
Vegetable oil for frying

1. Cut deep slit down back of each shrimp; press gently with fingers to flatten.

2. Whisk egg, cornstarch, salt and pepper in large bowl until blended. Add shrimp; toss to coat.

3. Drain each shrimp and press, cut side down, onto each piece of bread. Brush small amount of leftover egg mixture onto each shrimp.

4. Place 1 piece each of hard-cooked egg yolk, ham and chopped green onion on top of each shrimp.

5. Heat about 1 inch oil in large skillet over medium-high heat to 375°F. Add three or four bread pieces at a time; cook 1 to 2 minutes, then spoon hot oil over shrimp until shrimp are pink and opaque and toast is golden brown. Drain on paper towels.

southern pimiento cheese

Makes 2¼ cups spread

- 1 package (3 ounces) cream cheese, softened
- ⅓ cup HELLMANN'S® or BEST FOODS® Real Mayonnaise
- 2 cups shredded Cheddar cheese (about 8 ounces)
- ½ cup drained and chopped pimientos (about 4 ounces)
- ½ cup finely chopped green onions
- ¼ cup finely chopped pimiento-stuffed green olives
- 1 teaspoon garlic powder with parsley
- 1 teaspoon paprika

1. In medium bowl, with wire whisk, beat cream cheese and Hellmann's or Best Foods Real Mayonnaise until smooth. Stir in cheese, pimientos, green onions, olives, garlic powder with parsley and paprika until blended. Chill until ready to serve.

2. Serve at room temperature and, if desired, with crackers or party-size bread.

Prep Time: 15 minutes
Chill Time: 30 minutes

Tip: Pimientos are red, heart-shaped sweet peppers. They can be found diced in jars or stuffed inside green olives. When dried and ground, they become paprika, a colorful and sometimes spicy seasoning.

baked beer-battered onions and shrimp

Makes 4 to 6 servings

  4 tablespoons vegetable oil
  1 large Walla Walla or other sweet onion
  1 cup all-purpose flour, divided
  1 teaspoon salt, divided
  ¾ teaspoon ground red pepper, divided
  ½ cup lager beer
  1 egg
1½ cups panko or regular bread crumbs
  ¼ teaspoon black pepper
  1 pound large raw shrimp, peeled and deveined, with tails on
    Prepared dipping sauce (optional)

1. Preheat oven to 425°F. Spread 2 tablespoons oil on each of two baking sheets.

2. Slice onion into ½-inch circles and separate into rings, keeping only large whole rings (reserve remaining onion for another use).

3. Combine ¾ cup flour, ½ teaspoon salt and ½ teaspoon red pepper in medium bowl; mix well. Beat beer and egg in small bowl; stir into flour mixture.

4. Combine bread crumbs, remaining ¼ cup flour, ½ teaspoon salt, ¼ teaspoon red pepper and black pepper in resealable food storage bag. Dredge onion rings in beer batter. Place in bag and shake to coat. Spread on one prepared baking sheet. Repeat with shrimp and place on second baking sheet.

5. Bake onion rings 8 minutes. Turn rings over; bake 8 minutes. Bake shrimp on top rack 5 minutes. Turn shrimp over; bake 5 minutes. Serve hot with dipping sauce, if desired.

15 - Shindig Starters

baked beer-battered onions and shrimp

crab canapés

Makes about 16 servings

⅔ cup cream cheese, softened
2 teaspoons lemon juice
1 teaspoon hot pepper sauce
1 package (8 ounces) imitation crabmeat or lobster, flaked
⅓ cup chopped red bell pepper
2 green onions, sliced (about ¼ cup)
3 medium cucumbers, cut into ⅜-inch-thick slices
Chopped fresh parsley (optional)

1. Combine cream cheese, lemon juice and hot pepper sauce in medium bowl; mix well. Stir in crabmeat, bell pepper and green onions. Cover and refrigerate at least 1 hour.

2. To serve, spoon crabmeat mixture evenly onto each cucumber slice. Garnish with parsley.

lemon herbal iced tea

Makes 4 (8-ounce) servings

2 SUNKIST® lemons
4 cups boiling water
6 herbal tea bags (peppermint and spearmint blend or ginger-flavored)
Ice cubes
Honey or sugar to taste

With vegetable peeler, peel each lemon in continuous spiral, removing only outer colored layer of peel (save peeled fruit for other uses). In large pitcher, pour boiling water over tea bags and lemon peel. Cover and steep 10 minutes. Remove tea bags; chill tea mixture with peel in covered container. To serve, remove peel and pour over ice cubes in tall glasses. Sweeten to taste with honey. Garnish with lemon half-cartwheel slices, if desired.

17 - SHINDIG STARTERS

crab canapés

sweet potato fries

Makes 3 servings

1 teaspoon kosher salt
¼ teaspoon *each* black pepper and ground red pepper
2 large sweet potatoes, peeled and cut into thin spears
2 tablespoons vegetable oil

1. Preheat oven to 425°F. Line two baking sheets with foil; spray with nonstick cooking spray. Combine salt, black pepper and red pepper in small bowl; set aside.

2. Place sweet potato spears and oil in large bowl; toss well to coat. Arrange sweet potatoes on prepared baking sheets in single layer.

3. Bake 30 minutes or until lightly browned and crisp, turning potatoes once. Toss hot fries with seasoning mixture. Serve immediately.

pineapple-mint lemonade

Makes 8 servings

1 cup sugar
⅔ cup water
⅓ cup chopped fresh mint
1 can (46 ounces) DOLE® Pineapple Juice
1 cup lemon juice
Fresh mint sprigs (optional)

• Combine sugar and water in large saucepan; bring to boil. Boil 1 minute; remove from heat. Stir in chopped mint; let stand 15 minutes.

• Strain liquid into punch bowl; discard chopped mint. Add pineapple and lemon juice. Serve over ice cubes in tall glasses. Garnish with mint sprigs, if desired.

Summer Spritzer: Combine 2 cups Pineapple-Mint Lemonade with 2 cups mineral or sparkling water. Serve over ice. Makes 4 servings.

Prep Time: 15 minutes
Cook/Stand Time: 20 minutes

sweet potato fries

fried green tomatoes

Makes 3 to 4 servings

¼ cup all-purpose flour
¼ cup yellow cornmeal
½ teaspoon salt
½ teaspoon garlic salt
½ teaspoon ground red pepper
½ teaspoon black pepper
1 cup buttermilk
1 cup vegetable oil
2 medium green tomatoes, cut into ¼-inch-thick slices
   Shredded lettuce (optional)
   Hot pepper sauce (optional)

1. Combine flour, cornmeal, salt, garlic salt, red pepper and black pepper in pie plate or shallow bowl; mix well. Pour buttermilk into second pie plate or shallow bowl.

2. Heat oil in large skillet over medium heat. Dip tomato slices into buttermilk, coating both sides. Immediately dredge slices in flour mixture; shake off excess flour mixture.

3. Cook tomato slices in hot oil 3 to 5 minutes per side. Drain on paper towels. Serve immediately with lettuce and hot pepper sauce, if desired.

Tip: For additional flavor, heat 2 tablespoons of bacon grease with the vegetable oil.

fried green tomatoes

savory corn cakes

Makes 12 cakes

2 cups all-purpose flour
1 teaspoon baking powder
½ teaspoon salt
2 cups frozen corn, thawed
1 cup (4 ounces) shredded smoked Cheddar cheese
1 cup milk
2 egg whites, beaten
1 egg, beaten
4 green onions, finely chopped
2 cloves garlic, minced
1 tablespoon chili powder
2 tablespoons vegetable oil
Salsa (optional)

1. Combine flour, baking powder and salt in large bowl. Add corn, cheese, milk, egg whites, egg, green onions, garlic and chili powder; stir until well blended.

2. Heat oil in large skillet over medium-high heat. Drop batter by ¼ cupfuls into skillet. Cook 3 minutes per side or until golden brown. Serve with salsa, if desired.

27 - Homestyle Breads

savory corn cakes

honey sweet potato biscuits

Makes 10 biscuits

2 cups all-purpose flour
1 tablespoon baking powder
½ teaspoon salt
¼ cup vegetable shortening
1 tablespoon grated orange peel
1 tablespoon grated lemon peel
¾ cup mashed cooked sweet potato (1 large sweet potato baked until tender, peeled and mashed)
⅓ cup honey
½ cup milk

Combine flour, baking powder and salt in large bowl. Cut in shortening until mixture is size of small peas. Add orange and lemon peels, sweet potato and honey; mix well. Add enough milk to make soft, but not sticky, dough. Knead 3 or 4 times on lightly floured surface. Pat dough to 1-inch thickness and cut into 2¼-inch rounds; place on ungreased baking sheet.

Bake in preheated 400°F oven 15 to 18 minutes or until lightly browned. Serve warm.

Favorite recipe from National Honey Board

honey sweet potato biscuits

bayou yam muffins

Makes 12 muffins

 1 cup flour
 1 cup yellow cornmeal
 ¼ cup sugar
 1 tablespoon baking powder
 1¼ teaspoons ground cinnamon
 ½ teaspoon salt
 2 eggs
 1 cup mashed yams or sweet potatoes
 ½ cup very strong cold coffee
 ¼ cup (½ stick) butter or margarine, melted
 ½ teaspoon Original TABASCO® brand Pepper Sauce

Preheat oven to 425°F. Grease 12 (3×1½-inch) muffin cups. Combine flour, cornmeal, sugar, baking powder, cinnamon and salt in large bowl. Beat eggs in medium bowl; stir in yams, coffee, butter and TABASCO® Sauce. Make a well in center of dry ingredients; add yam mixture and stir just to combine. Spoon batter into prepared muffin cups. Bake 20 to 25 minutes or until cake tester inserted in center of muffin comes out clean. Cool 5 minutes on wire rack. Remove from pans. Serve warm or at room temperature.

Microwave Directions: Prepare muffin batter as directed above. Spoon approximately ⅓ cup batter into each of 6 paper baking cup-lined 6-ounce custard cups or microwave-safe muffin pan cups. Cook uncovered on HIGH (100% power) 4 to 5½ minutes or until cake tester inserted in center of muffin comes out clean; turn and rearrange cups or turn muffin pan ½ turn once during cooking. Remove muffins with small spatula. Cool 5 minutes on wire rack. Remove from pans. Repeat procedure with remaining batter. Serve warm or at room temperature.

spinach spoon bread

Makes 8 servings

- 1 package (10 ounces) frozen chopped spinach, thawed and squeezed dry
- 1 red bell pepper, diced
- 4 eggs, lightly beaten
- 1 cup cottage cheese
- 1 package (5½ ounces) corn bread mix
- 6 green onions, sliced
- ½ cup (1 stick) butter, melted
- 1¼ teaspoons seasoned salt

Slow Cooker Directions

1. Lightly grease slow cooker. Turn heat to HIGH.

2. Combine spinach, bell pepper, eggs, cottage cheese, corn bread mix, green onions, butter and salt in large bowl; mix well. Pour batter into prepared slow cooker. Place lid on slow cooker slightly ajar to allow excess moisture to escape. Cook on LOW 3 to 4 hours or on HIGH 1¾ to 2 hours or until edges are golden and knife inserted into center comes out clean.

3. To serve, scoop bread from slow cooker with spoon. Or, loosen edges and bottom with knife and invert onto plate; cut into wedges.

sawmill biscuits and gravy

◦❧ *Makes 8 servings* ❧◦

   3 tablespoons vegetable oil, divided
   8 ounces bulk breakfast sausage
   2¼ cups plus 3 tablespoons biscuit baking mix, divided
   2⅔ cups whole milk, divided
   Salt and black pepper

1. Preheat oven to 450°F. Heat 1 tablespoon oil in large nonstick skillet over medium heat. Add sausage; cook until browned, stirring to break up meat. Remove to plate with slotted spoon; set aside.

2. Add remaining 2 tablespoons oil to skillet. Add 3 tablespoons biscuit mix; whisk until smooth. Gradually stir in 2 cups milk; cook and stir 3 to 4 minutes or until mixture comes to a boil. Cook 1 minute or until thickened, stirring constantly. Stir in sausage and any juices; cook and stir 2 minutes. Season with salt and pepper. Keep warm.

3. Combine remaining 2¼ cups biscuit mix and ⅔ cup milk in medium bowl. Spoon 8 mounds onto ungreased nonstick baking sheet.

4. Bake 8 to 10 minutes or until golden brown. Serve warm with gravy.

33 - Homestyle Breads

sawmill biscuits and gravy

mini corn bread muffins

~ *Makes 24 mini muffins* ~

1 cup stone ground cornmeal*
¾ cup all-purpose flour
2 tablespoons sugar
¾ teaspoon baking powder
½ teaspoon baking soda
½ teaspoon salt
1 cup buttermilk
1 egg
3 tablespoons canola oil

*Stone ground cornmeal makes muffins with a rustic, authentic taste, and is found in grocery stores and health food stores.

1. Preheat oven to 375°F. Spray 24 mini (1¾-inch) muffin cups with nonstick cooking spray.

2. Mix cornmeal, flour, sugar, baking powder, baking soda and salt in large bowl. Mix buttermilk, egg and oil in medium bowl. Add to flour mixture; stir just until blended. Spoon batter into prepared muffin cups.

3. Bake 13 to 15 minutes or until lightly browned and toothpick inserted into centers comes out clean.

mini corn bread muffins

green onion cream cheese breakfast biscuits

Makes 8 biscuits

2 cups all-purpose flour
1 tablespoon baking powder
1 tablespoon sugar
¾ teaspoon salt
1 package (3 ounces) cream cheese
¼ cup shortening
½ cup finely chopped green onions
⅔ cup milk

1. Preheat oven to 450°F.

2. Combine flour, baking powder, sugar and salt in medium bowl. Cut in cream cheese and shortening with pastry blender or two knives until mixture resembles coarse crumbs. Stir in green onions.

3. Make well in center of flour mixture. Add milk; stir until mixture forms soft dough that clings together and forms a ball.

4. Turn out dough onto well-floured surface. Knead dough gently 10 to 12 times. Roll or pat dough to ½-inch thickness. Cut dough with floured 3-inch biscuit cutter. Place biscuits 2 inches apart on ungreased baking sheet.

5. Bake 10 to 12 minutes or until golden brown. Serve warm.

Tip: There are two keys to making fluffy, tender biscuits. One is to cut the chilled shortening or butter into the dry ingredients just until the mixture forms coarse crumbs. Blending any further will produce mealy biscuits. The second key is to work with the biscuit dough quickly and gently. Overworking the dough makes the biscuits tough.

green onion cream cheese breakfast biscuits

dinner rolls

Makes 24 rolls

1¼ cups milk
½ cup shortening
3¾ to 4¼ cups all-purpose flour, divided
¼ cup sugar
2 packages (¼ ounce each) active dry yeast
1 teaspoon salt
2 eggs

1. Combine milk and shortening in small saucepan. Heat over low heat until temperature reaches 120° to 130°F. (Shortening does not need to melt completely.) Combine 1½ cups flour, sugar, yeast and salt in large bowl. Gradually beat milk mixture into flour mixture with electric mixer at low speed. Beat in eggs and 1 cup flour. Beat at medium speed 2 minutes. Stir in enough additional flour, about 1¼ cups, with wooden spoon to make soft dough.

2. Turn out dough onto lightly floured surface. Knead in enough remaining flour to make smooth and elastic dough, about 10 minutes. Place dough in large, lightly greased bowl; turn once to grease surface. Cover with towel; let rise in warm place 1 hour or until doubled.

3. Punch down dough. Knead on lightly floured surface 1 minute. Cover with towel; let rest 10 minutes. Grease two 8-inch square baking pans. Cut dough in half. Cut one half into 12 pieces, keeping remaining half covered with towel. Shape pieces into balls; place in rows in one prepared pan. Repeat with remaining dough. Cover pans with towels; let rise in warm place 30 minutes or until doubled.

4. Preheat oven to 375°F. Bake 15 to 20 minutes or until golden brown. Remove immediately from pans. Cool on wire racks. Serve warm.

southern spoon bread

Makes 6 servings

- 4 eggs, separated
- 3 cups milk
- 1 cup yellow cornmeal
- 3 tablespoons butter
- 1 teaspoon salt
- ¼ teaspoon black pepper *or* ⅛ teaspoon ground red pepper
- 1 teaspoon baking powder
- 1 tablespoon grated Parmesan cheese (optional)

1. Preheat oven to 375°F. Spray 2-quart round casserole with nonstick cooking spray. Beat egg yolks in small bowl; set aside.

2. Heat milk almost to a boil in medium saucepan over medium heat. Gradually beat in cornmeal using wire whisk. Cook 2 minutes, stirring constantly. Whisk in butter, salt and pepper. Beat about ¼ cup cornmeal mixture into egg yolks. Beat egg yolk mixture into remaining cornmeal mixture; set aside.

3. Beat egg whites in large bowl with electric mixer at high speed until stiff peaks form. Stir baking powder into cornmeal mixture. Stir about ¼ cup egg whites into cornmeal mixture. Gradually fold in remaining egg whites. Pour into prepared casserole; sprinkle with cheese, if desired.

4. Bake 30 to 35 minutes or until golden brown and toothpick inserted into center comes out clean. Serve immediately.

oaty pear 'n' pecan pancakes

Makes 12 pancakes

1 cup AUNT JEMIMA® Original Pancake Mix
1 teaspoon ground cinnamon
1 cup milk
1 egg
1 tablespoon vegetable oil
1 medium-firm ripe pear, cored and chopped (about 1 cup)
¾ cup QUAKER® Oats (quick or old fashioned, uncooked)
2 tablespoons chopped toasted pecans
½ to ¾ cup AUNT JEMIMA LITE® Syrup, warmed
Pear slices (optional)
Chopped toasted pecans (optional)

1. Stir together pancake mix and cinnamon in large bowl. Combine milk, egg and oil in medium bowl; mix well. Add to pancake mix; stir with wire whisk just until combined. Gently stir in pear, oats and 2 tablespoons pecans. Let stand 1 to 2 minutes to thicken.

2. Cook pancakes on hot griddle according to package directions. Serve with syrup and, if desired, pear slices and additional pecans.

Tip: To toast nuts, spread in single layer on cookie sheet. Bake at 350°F about 6 to 8 minutes or until lightly browned and fragrant, stirring occasionally. Cool before using. Or spread in single layer on microwave-safe plate. Microwave on HIGH (100% power) 1 minute; stir. Continue to microwave on HIGH, checking every 30 seconds, until nuts are fragrant and brown. Cool before using.

41 - Homestyle Breads

oaty pear 'n' pecan pancakes

sausage and cheddar corn bread

Makes 10 servings

  1 tablespoon vegetable oil
½ pound bulk pork sausage
  1 medium onion, diced
  1 jalapeño pepper,* diced
  1 package (8 ounces) corn muffin mix
  1 cup (4 ounces) shredded Cheddar cheese, divided
⅓ cup milk
  1 egg

*Jalapeño peppers can sting and irritate the skin, so wear rubber gloves when handling peppers and do not touch your eyes.

1. Heat oil in large cast iron skillet over medium heat. Brown sausage, stirring to break up meat. Add onion and jalapeño; cook and stir 5 minutes or until vegetables are softened. Remove sausage mixture to medium bowl.

2. Preheat oven to 350°F. Combine corn muffin mix, ½ cup cheese, milk and egg in separate medium bowl. Pour batter into skillet. Spread sausage mixture over top. Sprinkle with remaining ½ cup cheese.

3. Bake 20 to 25 minutes or until edges are lightly browned. Cut into wedges. Refrigerate leftovers.

sausage and cheddar corn bread

Soups 'n Gumbos

black-eyed pea soup

Makes 12 to 16 servings

2 large potatoes, peeled and grated
4 medium onions, thinly sliced
4 carrots, thinly sliced
½ pound bacon, diced
8 quarts (32 cups) water
2 pounds dried black-eyed peas, rinsed and sorted
2 cups thinly sliced celery
1 meaty ham bone
2 whole jalapeño peppers*
4 bay leaves
½ teaspoon dried thyme
Salt and black pepper

Jalapeño peppers can sting and irritate the skin, so wear rubber gloves when handling peppers and do not touch your eyes.

1. Place potatoes in large bowl of cold water; set aside.

2. Combine onions, carrots and bacon in large saucepan; cook and stir over medium-high heat until onions are golden.

3. Drain potatoes. Add potatoes, water, black-eyed peas, celery, ham bone, jalapeño peppers, bay leaves and thyme to onion mixture. Season with salt and black pepper. Reduce heat to low. Cover and simmer 3 to 4 hours. Remove and discard jalapeño peppers and bay leaves.

4. Remove ham bone; cool. Cut meat from bone; discard bone. Chop meat; stir into soup.

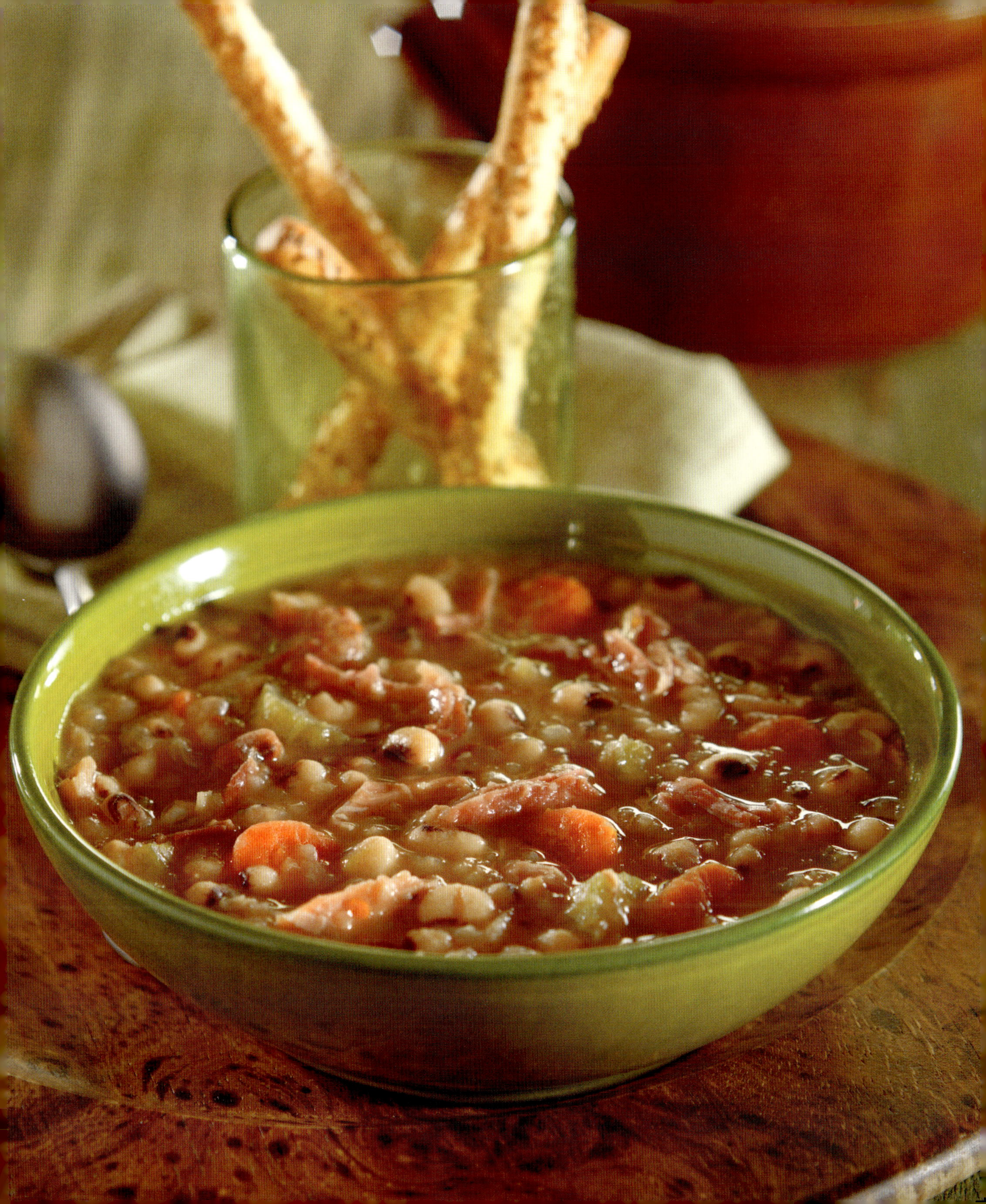

chicken & sausage gumbo

~ *Makes 6 servings* ~

2 tablespoons olive oil

2 skinless, boneless chicken breasts halves (about ½ pound), cut into 1-inch pieces

1 pound turkey kielbasa, cut into 1-inch pieces

1 large onion, finely chopped (about 1 cup)

1 large green or red pepper, diced (about 1⅓ cups)

2 stalks celery, diced (about 1 cup)

1 can (10¾ ounces) CAMPBELL'S® Condensed Cream of Chicken Soup (Regular or 98% Fat Free)

½ cup water

2 teaspoons hot pepper sauce

1 teaspoon gumbo filé powder

Hot cooked white rice

1. Heat 1 tablespoon oil in large skillet over medium-high heat. Add chicken and kielbasa in 2 batches and cook until browned, stirring often. Remove chicken and kielbasa.

2. Add remaining oil and heat over medium heat. Add onion, green pepper and celery and cook until tender.

3. Add soup, water, hot sauce and filé powder. Return chicken and kielbasa to skillet. Cover and cook over low heat 15 minutes. Serve over rice.

Prep Time: 15 minutes
Cook Time: 35 minutes
Total Time: 50 minutes

47 - Soups 'n Gumbos

chicken & sausage gumbo

thick and creamy succotash soup

~ *Makes 6 servings* ~

2 slices bacon
1 onion, chopped
1 stalk celery, chopped
2 tablespoons all-purpose flour
3 cups chicken broth
1½ cups corn
1 cup frozen baby lima beans, thawed
1 bay leaf
¼ teaspoon hot pepper sauce
Salt and black pepper
½ cup whipping cream

1. Cook bacon in Dutch oven over medium heat until crisp and browned. Drain on paper towels. Crumble and set aside.

2. Add onion and celery to bacon drippings in Dutch oven; cook and stir 5 minutes or until tender. Stir in flour; cook until slightly thickened. Stir in broth. Bring to a boil over high heat. Reduce heat to low; simmer until slightly thickened.

3. Stir in bacon, corn, lima beans, bay leaf, hot pepper sauce, salt and black pepper; simmer 15 minutes. Remove from heat; stir in cream. Remove and discard bay leaf.

> **Tip:** If preparing this soup in advance, cover and refrigerate up to 1 day. To serve, reheat over low heat. *Do not allow to boil.*

thick and creamy succotash soup

louisiana gumbo

Makes 6 servings

2 cups MINUTE® White Rice, uncooked
2 tablespoons butter
2 tablespoons all-purpose flour
½ cup onion, chopped
½ cup celery, chopped
½ cup green bell pepper, chopped
1 clove garlic, minced
1 package (14 ounces) smoked turkey sausage, sliced
1 can (14½ ounces) diced tomatoes
1 can (14½ ounces) chicken broth
1 package (10 ounces) frozen sliced okra, thawed*
1 tablespoon Cajun seasoning
¼ teaspoon dried thyme
½ pound shrimp, peeled, deveined
Salt and black pepper, to taste

Or substitute 1 package (10 ounces) frozen cut green beans.

Prepare rice according to package directions.

Melt butter in large skillet over medium-high heat. Stir in flour; cook and stir until light golden brown, about 5 minutes. Add onion, celery, bell pepper and garlic; cook 2 to 3 minutes or until tender.

Stir in sausage, tomatoes, broth, okra, seasoning and thyme; cover. Simmer 5 minutes, stirring occasionally.

Add shrimp; cook 5 minutes or until shrimp are pink. Season with salt and pepper to taste. Serve with rice.

51 - Soups 'n Gumbos

louisiana gumbo

charleston crab soup

~ *Makes 4 servings* ~

  8 ounces lump crabmeat, fresh, frozen or pasteurized
  2 tablespoons butter
  ½ cup finely chopped onion
  1 tablespoon plus 1½ teaspoons all-purpose flour
  1 cup bottled clam juice or chicken broth
  2½ cups half-and-half
  1½ teaspoons Worcestershire sauce
  ½ teaspoon salt
     Dash ground white pepper
  1 to 2 tablespoons dry sherry

1. Pick out and discard any shell or cartilage from crabmeat; set aside. Melt butter in medium saucepan over medium-low heat. Add onion; cook and stir 4 minutes or until tender. Stir in flour; cook and stir 1 minute.

2. Add clam juice; cook and stir over medium heat until mixture comes to a simmer. Add half-and-half, crabmeat, Worcestershire sauce, salt and pepper; cook and stir over low heat 3 to 4 minutes or just until mixture begins to simmer, stirring occasionally. Remove from heat; stir in sherry.

charleston crab soup

barley and sausage gumbo

Makes 4 servings

1 small onion, chopped
1 large green bell pepper, chopped
1 cup sliced okra
1 medium stalk celery, chopped
1 clove garlic, minced
1 cup chicken broth
1 cup tomato purée
¼ cup uncooked pearl barley
1 teaspoon dried oregano
¼ teaspoon salt
⅛ teaspoon red pepper flakes
2 chicken andouille sausages (3 ounces each), sliced ½ inch thick

Slow Cooker Directions

1. Place onion, bell pepper, okra, celery and garlic in slow cooker. Add broth, tomato purée, barley, oregano, salt and red pepper flakes; stir. Add sausages. Cover; cook on LOW 5 to 6 hours.

2. Let stand 5 minutes before serving.

> **Tip:** When selecting fresh okra, look for firm, brightly colored pods measuring under 4 inches in length. Longer pods are often tough and fibrous. Avoid pods that are dull, limp or blemished.

barley and sausage gumbo

red bean soup with andouille sausage

Makes 6 to 8 servings

- 2 tablespoons butter
- 1 large onion, diced
- 3 stalks celery, diced
- 2 cloves garlic, chopped
- 8 cups chicken broth
- 1½ cups dried red kidney beans, soaked in cold water 1 hour, rinsed and drained
- 1 ham hock
- 1 bay leaf
- 2 parsnips, diced
- 1 sweet potato, peeled and diced
- 1 pound andouille sausage or kielbasa, sliced ½ inch thick
- Salt and black pepper

Slow Cooker Directions

1. Melt butter in large saucepan over medium heat. Add onion, celery and garlic; cook and stir 5 minutes or until tender. Transfer to slow cooker; add broth, beans, ham hock and bay leaf. Cover; cook on HIGH 2 hours.

2. Remove ham hock; let stand until cool enough to handle. Remove ham from hock; discard bone. Chop ham and return to slow cooker. Add parsnips and sweet potato. Cover; cook on HIGH 2 hours.

3. Add sausage. Cover; cook on HIGH 30 minutes or until heated through. Remove and discard bay leaf. Season with salt and pepper.

new orleans pork gumbo

~ *Makes 4 servings* ~

Nonstick cooking spray
1 pound pork tenderloin, cut into ½-inch cubes
1 tablespoon butter
2 tablespoons all-purpose flour
1 cup water
1 can (about 14 ounces) stewed tomatoes
1 package (10 ounces) frozen cut okra
1 package (10 ounces) frozen succotash
1 beef bouillon cube
1 teaspoon black pepper
1 teaspoon hot pepper sauce
1 bay leaf

1. Spray large Dutch oven with cooking spray; heat over medium heat. Add pork; cook and stir 4 minutes or until pork is browned. Remove pork from Dutch oven.

2. Melt butter in same Dutch oven. Stir in flour; cook and stir until mixture is dark brown but not burned. Gradually whisk in water until smooth. Add pork, tomatoes, okra, succotash, bouillon cube, black pepper, hot pepper sauce and bay leaf; bring to a boil. Reduce heat to low; simmer 15 minutes. Remove and discard bay leaf.

cajun-style chicken soup

Makes 6 servings

1½ pounds chicken thighs
4 cups chicken broth
1 can (8 ounces) tomato sauce
1 medium onion, chopped
2 stalks celery, sliced
2 cloves garlic, minced
2 bay leaves
1 teaspoon salt
½ teaspoon ground cumin
¼ teaspoon paprika
¼ teaspoon ground red pepper
¼ teaspoon black pepper
Dash white pepper
1 large green bell pepper, chopped
⅓ cup uncooked rice
8 ounces fresh or frozen okra, cut into ½-inch slices
Hot pepper sauce (optional)

1. Place chicken, broth, tomato sauce, onion, celery, garlic, bay leaves, salt, cumin, paprika, red pepper, black pepper and white pepper in 5-quart Dutch oven; bring to a boil over high heat. Reduce heat to medium-low. Simmer, uncovered, 1 hour or until chicken is cooked through (165°F), skimming foam that rises to the surface.

2. Remove chicken; cool slightly. Skim fat from soup. Remove chicken meat from bones; discard skin and bones. Cut chicken into bite-size pieces.

3. Add chicken, bell pepper and rice to soup; bring to a boil. Reduce heat; simmer 12 minutes or until rice is tender. Add okra; simmer 8 minutes or until okra is tender. Remove and discard bay leaves. Serve with hot pepper sauce, if desired.

cajun-style chicken soup

spicy shrimp gumbo

Makes 8 servings

½ cup vegetable oil
½ cup all-purpose flour
1 large onion, chopped
½ cup chopped fresh parsley
½ cup chopped celery
½ cup sliced green onions
6 cloves garlic, minced
4 cups chicken broth or water
1 package (10 ounces) frozen sliced okra, thawed
1 teaspoon salt
½ teaspoon ground red pepper
2 pounds medium raw shrimp, peeled and deveined
3 cups hot cooked rice
Fresh parsley sprigs (optional)

1. Combine oil and flour in large heavy saucepan; cook over medium heat 10 to 15 minutes or until mixture is dark brown but not burned, stirring often.

2. Add onion, chopped parsley, celery, green onions and garlic to flour mixture; cook 5 to 10 minutes or until vegetables are tender. Add broth, okra, salt and red pepper; cover and simmer 15 minutes.

3. Add shrimp; simmer 3 to 5 minutes or until shrimp turn pink and opaque.

4. Serve rice over gumbo. Garnish with parsley sprigs.

63 - Soups 'n Gumbos

spicy shrimp gumbo

Hearty Meat Dishes

spicy buttermilk oven-fried chicken

Makes 6 servings

3½ pounds whole chicken, cut up
2 cups buttermilk
1½ cups all-purpose flour
1 teaspoon salt
1 teaspoon ground red pepper
½ teaspoon garlic powder
¼ cup canola oil

1. Place chicken pieces in single layer in 13×9-inch baking dish. Pour buttermilk over chicken. Cover with plastic wrap; refrigerate at least 2 hours.

2. Preheat oven to 350°F. Combine flour, salt, red pepper and garlic powder in large shallow bowl. Heat oil in large skillet over medium-high heat.

3. Remove chicken from buttermilk; discard buttermilk. Coat chicken with flour mixture. Place chicken in hot oil; cook about 10 minutes or until brown and crisp on all sides. Place chicken back into clean baking dish. Bake 30 to 45 minutes or until chicken is cooked through (165°F).

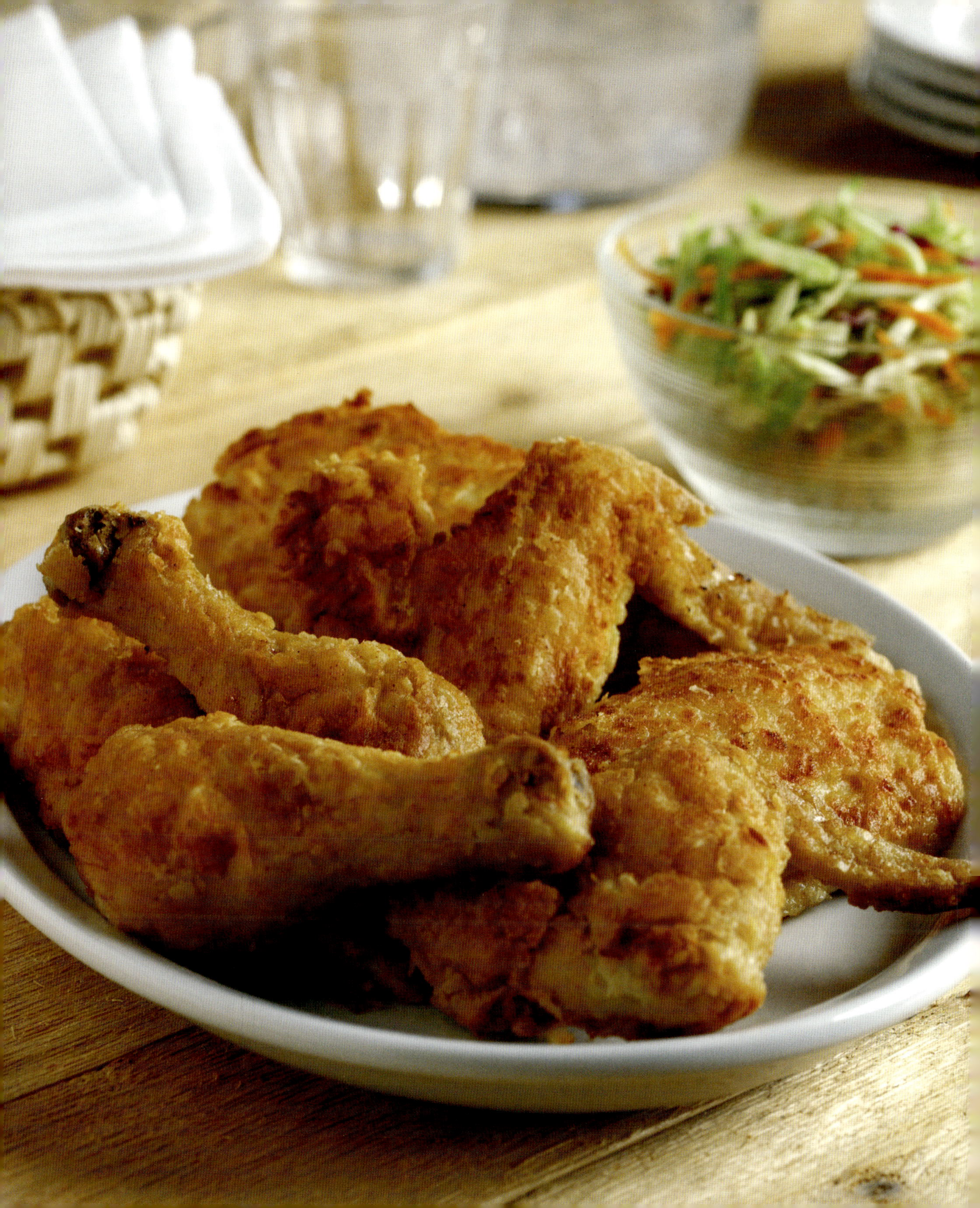

pork and corn bread stuffing casserole

Makes 4 servings

½ teaspoon paprika
¼ teaspoon salt
¼ teaspoon garlic powder
¼ teaspoon black pepper
4 bone-in pork chops (about 1¾ pounds)
2 tablespoons butter
1½ cups chopped onions
¾ cup thinly sliced celery
¾ cup matchstick or shredded carrots
¼ cup chopped fresh Italian parsley
1 can (about 14 ounces) chicken broth
4 cups corn bread stuffing mix

1. Preheat oven to 350°F. Lightly coat 13×9-inch baking dish with nonstick cooking spray.

2. Combine paprika, salt, garlic powder and pepper in small bowl. Sprinkle over both sides of pork chops.

3. Melt butter in large skillet over medium-high heat. Add pork chops; cook 4 minutes or just until browned, turning once. Transfer to plate.

4. Add onions, celery, carrots and parsley to same skillet; cook and stir 4 minutes or until onions are translucent. Add broth; bring to a boil. Remove from heat; add stuffing mix and fluff with fork.

5. Transfer stuffing mixture to prepared baking dish. Top with pork chops. Bake, covered, 25 minutes or until pork is barely pink in center.

pork and corn bread stuffing casserole

grilled muffuletta

Makes 4 sandwiches

4 round hard rolls, split
2 tablespoons vinaigrette salad dressing
⅓ cup olive salad or tapenade
6 ounces thinly sliced Genoa salami
6 ounces thinly sliced ham
6 ounces thinly sliced provolone cheese
Olive oil

1. Brush insides of rolls with salad dressing. Layer half of olive salad, salami, ham, cheese and remaining olive salad on roll bottoms; close sandwiches with roll tops. Brush outsides of sandwiches lightly with oil.

2. Heat large grill pan or nonstick skillet over medium heat. Add sandwiches; press down lightly with spatula or weigh down with small plate. Cook sandwiches 4 to 5 minutes per side or until cheese melts and sandwiches are golden brown.

hoppin' john

Makes 8 servings

1 package (14 ounces) smoked turkey sausage, thinly sliced
3 cans (15½ ounces each) black-eyed peas, drained, rinsed
2 cans (14½ ounces each) chicken broth
2 cups onions, chopped
1 teaspoon crushed red pepper
½ teaspoon ground red pepper
2½ cups MINUTE® White Rice, uncooked
Fresh parsley, chopped (optional)

Brown sausage in medium saucepan over medium-high heat. Add peas, broth, onions and seasonings; bring to a boil. Stir in rice; cover. Simmer 10 minutes or until rice is tender. Garnish with parsley, if desired.

69 - HEARTY MEAT DISHES

grilled muffuletta

southern country chicken and biscuits

◈ *Makes 4 servings* ◈

2 frozen boneless skinless chicken breasts
12 ounces new potatoes, scrubbed and diced
½ cup frozen green peas
1 jar (4 ounces) diced pimientos, drained
¼ teaspoon dried thyme
Salt and black pepper
1 can (10¾ ounces) condensed cream of chicken soup, undiluted
1 can (8-count) refrigerated biscuits

1. Place chicken, potatoes, peas, pimientos, thyme, salt and pepper in Dutch oven. Spoon soup over top of mixture. Bring to a boil over medium-high heat. Reduce heat; cover and simmer 40 minutes or until chicken is no longer pink in center, turning occasionally.

2. Meanwhile, bake biscuits according to package directions.

3. Shred chicken with two forks. Split biscuits; place in shallow bowls. Serve chicken, vegetables and sauce over biscuits.

HEARTY MEAT DISHES - 73

southern country chicken and biscuits

cajun-style beef and beans

Makes 6 servings

- 1 pound ground beef
- ¾ cup chopped onion
- 2½ cups cooked brown rice
- 1 can (about 15 ounces) kidney beans, rinsed and drained
- 1 can (about 14 ounces) stewed tomatoes
- 2 teaspoons Cajun Seasoning (recipe follows)
- ¾ cup (3 ounces) shredded Cheddar cheese

1. Preheat oven to 350°F.

2. Brown beef 6 to 8 minutes in large nonstick skillet over medium-high heat, stirring to break up meat. Drain fat. Add onion; cook and stir 2 minutes or until translucent. Combine beef mixture, rice, beans, tomatoes and Cajun Seasoning in 2- to 2½-quart casserole.

3. Bake, covered, 25 to 30 minutes, stirring once. Sprinkle with cheese; cover and let stand 5 minutes before serving.

cajun seasoning

Makes 1¾ cups

- ½ cup salt (optional)
- ¼ cup plus 1 tablespoon ground red pepper
- 3 tablespoons black pepper
- 3 tablespoons onion powder
- 3 tablespoons garlic powder
- 3 tablespoons chili powder
- 1 tablespoon dried thyme
- 1 tablespoon dried basil
- 1 tablespoon ground bay leaf

Combine all ingredients in medium bowl until well combined. Store in tightly sealed container.

cajun-style beef and beans

carolina-style barbecue chicken

Makes 8 servings

- 2 pounds boneless skinless chicken breasts
- ¾ cup packed light brown sugar, divided
- ¾ cup FRENCH'S® Classic Yellow® Mustard
- ½ cup cider vinegar
- ¼ cup FRANK'S® REDHOT® Original Cayenne Pepper Sauce
- 2 tablespoons vegetable oil
- 2 tablespoons FRENCH'S® Worcestershire Sauce
- ½ teaspoon salt
- ¼ teaspoon black pepper

1. Place chicken in large resealable plastic food storage bag. Combine ½ cup brown sugar, mustard, vinegar, Frank's RedHot Sauce, oil, Worcestershire, salt and pepper in 4-cup measure; mix well. Pour 1 cup mustard mixture over chicken. Seal bag; marinate in refrigerator 1 hour or overnight.

2. Pour remaining mustard mixture into small saucepan. Stir in remaining ¼ cup brown sugar. Bring to a boil. Reduce heat; simmer 5 minutes or until sugar dissolves and mixture thickens slightly, stirring often. Reserve for serving sauce.

3. Place chicken on well-oiled grid, reserving marinade. Grill over high heat 10 to 15 minutes or until chicken is no longer pink in center, turning and basting once with marinade. *Do not baste during last 5 minutes of cooking.* Discard any remaining marinade. Serve chicken with reserved sauce.

Prep Time: 15 minutes
Marinate Time: 1 hour
Cook Time: 10 minutes

chicken étouffé with pasta

Makes 6 servings

- ¼ cup vegetable oil
- ⅓ cup all-purpose flour
- ½ cup finely chopped onion
- 4 boneless skinless chicken breasts (about 1¼ pounds), cut into ¼-inch-thick strips
- 1 cup chicken broth
- 1 medium tomato, chopped
- ¾ cup sliced celery
- 1 medium green bell pepper, chopped
- 2 teaspoons Cajun or Creole seasoning
- Hot cooked pasta

1. Heat oil in large skillet over medium heat. Add flour; cook and stir 10 minutes or until dark brown. Add onion; cook and stir 2 minutes.

2. Stir in chicken, broth, tomato, celery, bell pepper and Cajun seasoning; cook 8 minutes or until chicken is cooked through. Serve over pasta.

Note: Étouffé is a traditional dish from New Orleans. This Cajun stew usually features chicken or shellfish, bell peppers, onions and celery.

smoky barbecued beef sandwiches

Makes 6 sandwiches

2 onions, thinly sliced and separated into rings
1 beef brisket (about 3 pounds), trimmed
½ teaspoon salt
¾ cup beer (not dark)
½ cup packed light brown sugar
½ cup ketchup
1 tablespoon plus 1½ teaspoons Worcestershire sauce
1 tablespoon plus 1½ teaspoons soy sauce
2 cloves garlic, minced
2 whole canned chipotle peppers in adobo sauce, finely chopped
1 to 3 teaspoons adobo sauce from can
6 hoagie or Kaiser rolls, split and toasted

1. Preheat oven to 325°F. Place onions in bottom of large roasting pan.

2. Place brisket, fat side up, over onions; sprinkle with salt. Combine beer, brown sugar, ketchup, Worcestershire sauce, soy sauce, garlic, chipotle peppers and adobo sauce in medium bowl; pour over brisket.

3. Bake, covered, 3 to 3½ hours or until brisket is fork-tender.

4. Transfer brisket to cutting board; tent with foil. Let stand 10 minutes. (Brisket and sauce may be prepared ahead to this point; cool and cover separately. Refrigerate up to 1 day before reheating and serving.)

5. Skim fat from pan juices with large spoon; discard fat. Transfer juices to large saucepan; cook over medium heat until thickened, stirring frequently.

6. Trim fat from brisket; carve brisket across the grain into thin slices. Return slices to sauce; cook until heated through, coating slices with sauce. Serve slices and sauce in rolls.

79 - Hearty Meat Dishes

smoky barbecued beef sandwich

cajun sausage and rice

Makes 5 servings

8 ounces kielbasa, cut into ¼-inch slices
1 can (about 14 ounces) diced tomatoes
1 medium onion, diced
1 medium green bell pepper, diced
2 stalks celery, thinly sliced
1 tablespoon chicken bouillon granules
1 tablespoon steak sauce
3 bay leaves *or* 1 teaspoon dried thyme
1 teaspoon sugar
¼ to ½ teaspoon hot pepper sauce
1 cup uncooked instant rice
½ cup water
½ cup chopped fresh parsley (optional)

Slow Cooker Directions

1. Combine sausage, tomatoes, onion, bell pepper, celery, bouillon, steak sauce, bay leaves, sugar and hot pepper sauce in slow cooker. Cover; cook on LOW 8 hours or on HIGH 4 hours.

2. Remove and discard bay leaves. Stir in rice and water. *Increase temperature to HIGH.* Cook on HIGH 25 minutes or until rice is tender. Stir in parsley, if desired.

Tip: Kielbasa is also called Polish sausage. It is usually made of pork and flavored with garlic. It comes in thick links and is most often smoked.

cajun sausage and rice

ham & barbecued bean skillet

Makes 4 servings

- 1 tablespoon vegetable oil
- 1 cup chopped onion
- 1 teaspoon minced garlic
- 1 can (about 15 ounces) kidney beans, rinsed and drained
- 1 can (about 15 ounces) cannellini or Great Northern beans, rinsed and drained
- 1 ham steak (½ inch thick, about 12 ounces), trimmed of fat and cut into ½-inch pieces
- 1 cup chopped green bell pepper
- ½ cup packed light brown sugar
- ½ cup ketchup
- 2 tablespoons cider vinegar
- 2 teaspoons dry mustard

1. Heat oil in large deep skillet over medium-high heat. Add onion and garlic; cook and stir 3 minutes. Add kidney beans, cannellini beans, ham, bell pepper, brown sugar, ketchup, vinegar and mustard; mix well.

2. Reduce heat to low; simmer 5 minutes or until sauce thickens and mixture is heated through, stirring occasionally.

Serving Suggestions: Serve with a Caesar salad and breadsticks.

83 - Hearty Meat Dishes

ham & barbecued bean skillet

Fish 'n Seafood

southern crab cakes with rémoulade dipping sauce

Makes 8 servings

- 10 ounces fresh lump crabmeat
- 1½ cups fresh white or sourdough bread crumbs, divided
- ½ cup mayonnaise, divided
- ¼ cup chopped green onions
- 1 egg white, lightly beaten
- 2 tablespoons coarse-grained or spicy brown mustard, divided
- ¾ teaspoon hot pepper sauce, divided
- 2 tablespoons olive oil, divided
- Lemon wedges (optional)

1. Pick out and discard any shell or cartilage from crabmeat. Combine crabmeat, ¾ cup bread crumbs, ¼ cup mayonnaise, green onions, egg white, 1 tablespoon mustard and ½ teaspoon hot pepper sauce in medium bowl; mix well. Shape into 8 (½-inch-thick) cakes. Roll crab cakes lightly in remaining ¾ cup bread crumbs.

2. Heat 1 tablespoon oil in large nonstick skillet over medium heat. Add 4 crab cakes; cook 4 to 5 minutes per side or until golden brown. Transfer to serving platter; keep warm. Repeat with remaining 1 tablespoon oil and crab cakes.

3. Combine remaining ¼ cup mayonnaise, 1 tablespoon mustard and ¼ teaspoon hot pepper sauce in small bowl; mix well. Serve crab cakes with dipping sauce and lemon wedges, if desired.

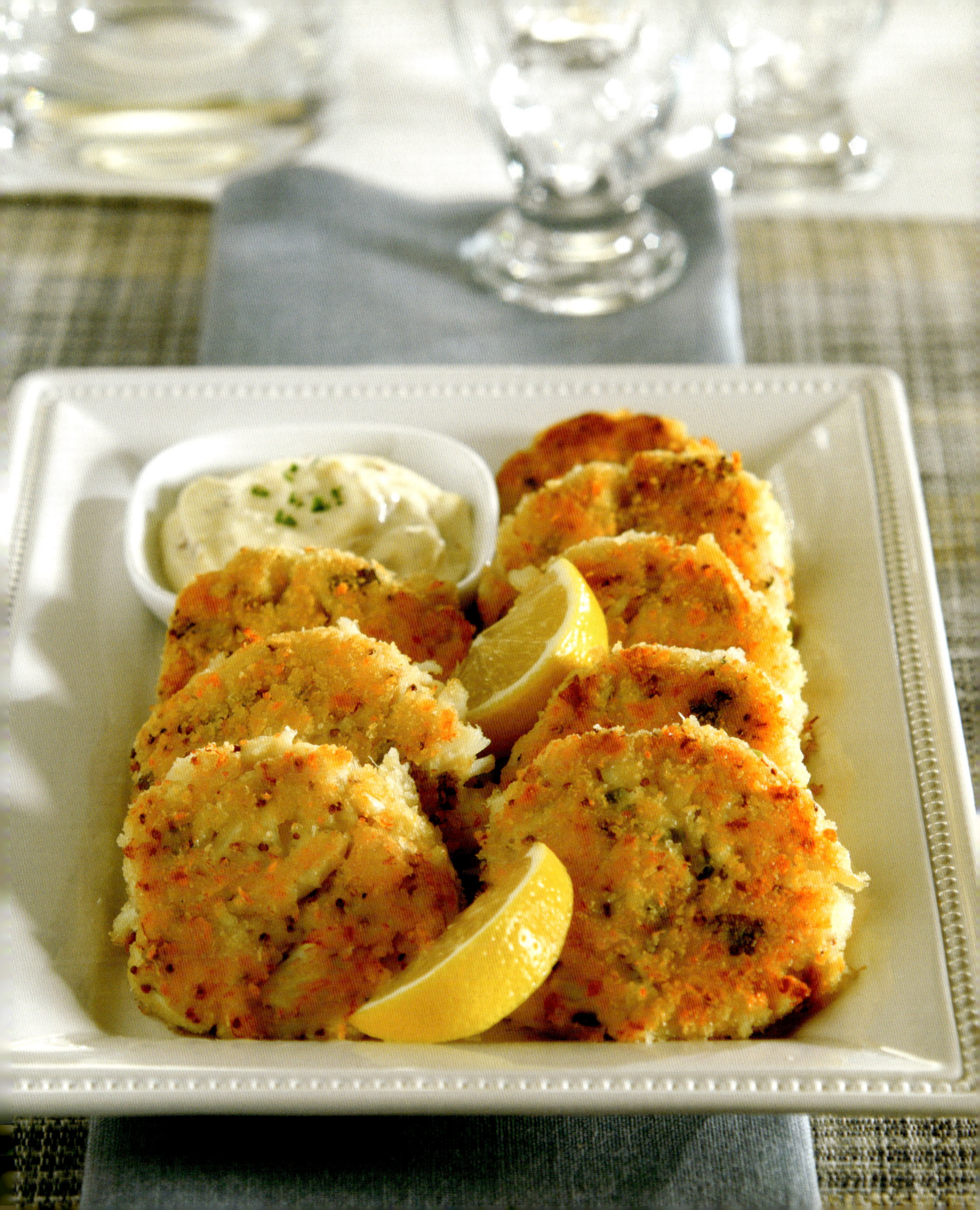

jambalaya

Makes 6 to 8 servings

1 package (16 ounces) Cajun sausage, sliced
1 cup chopped onion
1 cup chopped green bell pepper
2 cloves garlic, minced
2 cups uncooked rice
2 cups chicken broth
1 bottle (12 ounces) light-colored beer, such as pale ale
1 can (about 14 ounces) diced tomatoes with green pepper, onion and celery
1 teaspoon Cajun seasoning
1 pound medium cooked shrimp, peeled and deveined
   Chopped fresh parsley (optional)
   Hot pepper sauce (optional)

1. Brown sausage in large Dutch oven over medium-high heat; drain fat. Add onion, bell pepper and garlic; cook and stir 2 to 3 minutes or until tender. Add rice, broth and beer; cover and bring to a boil. Reduce heat to low. Simmer 20 minutes, stirring occasionally.

2. Stir in tomatoes and Cajun seasoning; cook 5 minutes. Add shrimp; cook 2 to 3 minutes or until heated through. Sprinkle with parsley and hot pepper sauce, if desired.

Tip: To peel shrimp, remove the legs by gently pulling them off the shell. Loosen the shell with your fingers, then slide it off. To devein shrimp, make a small cut along the back and lift out the dark vein with the tip of a knife. You may find this task easier to do under cold running water.

87 - Fish 'n' Seafood

jambalaya

broiled cajun fish fillets

Makes 4 servings

2 tablespoons all-purpose flour
½ cup seasoned dried bread crumbs
1 teaspoon dried thyme
½ teaspoon garlic salt
¼ teaspoon ground red pepper
¼ teaspoon black pepper
1 egg
1 tablespoon milk or water
4 scrod or orange roughy fillets, ½ inch thick (4 to 5 ounces each)
2 tablespoons butter, melted, divided
⅓ cup mayonnaise
2 tablespoons sweet pickle relish
1 tablespoon lemon juice
1 teaspoon prepared horseradish

1. Preheat broiler. Spray baking sheet with nonstick cooking spray.

2. Place flour in large resealable food storage bag. Combine bread crumbs, thyme, garlic salt, red pepper and black pepper in medium bowl. Whisk egg and milk in separate medium bowl.

3. Place fillets, one at a time, in flour; shake bag to coat lightly. Dip fillets into egg mixture, letting excess drip back into bowl. Place fillets in bread crumb mixture; turn to coat. Transfer fillets to prepared baking sheet. Brush 1 tablespoon butter evenly over fillets.

4. Broil 4 to 5 inches from heat 3 minutes. Turn fish; brush with remaining 1 tablespoon butter. Broil 3 minutes or until fish begins to flake when tested with fork.

5. Meanwhile, combine mayonnaise, relish, lemon juice and horseradish in small bowl; mix well. Serve with fish.

Note: You can prepare the tartar sauce in advance. Cover and refrigerate up to 1 day before serving. Stir lightly before serving.

broiled cajun fish fillets

shrimp creole

Makes 4 to 6 servings

    2 tablespoons olive oil
1½ cups chopped green bell peppers
    1 medium onion, chopped
   ⅔ cup chopped celery
    2 cloves garlic, minced
    1 cup uncooked rice
    1 can (about 14 ounces) diced tomatoes, drained and liquid reserved
    2 teaspoons hot pepper sauce
    1 teaspoon dried oregano
   ¾ teaspoon salt
   ½ teaspoon dried thyme
      Black pepper
    1 pound medium raw shrimp, peeled
    1 tablespoon chopped fresh parsley (optional)

1. Preheat oven to 325°F.

2. Heat oil in large skillet over medium-high heat. Add bell peppers, onion, celery and garlic; cook and stir 5 minutes or until vegetables are tender. Reduce heat to medium. Add rice; cook and stir 5 minutes. Add tomatoes, hot pepper sauce, oregano, salt, thyme and black pepper to skillet; stir until well blended.

3. Pour reserved tomato liquid into measuring cup. Add enough water to measure 1¾ cups. Add tomato liquid to skillet; cook and stir 2 minutes. Transfer mixture to 2½-quart casserole. Stir in shrimp.

4. Bake, covered, 55 minutes or until rice is tender and liquid is absorbed. Garnish with parsley.

oyster po' boys

Makes 4 sandwiches

    Spicy Mayonnaise (recipe follows)
¾ cup cornmeal
¼ cup all-purpose flour
    Salt and black pepper
¾ cup vegetable oil
2 pints shucked oysters, drained
4 French bread rolls,* split
    Lettuce leaves
    Tomato slices

*Substitute French bread loaf, split and cut into 4-inch lengths, for French bread rolls.

1. Prepare Spicy Mayonnaise.
2. Combine cornmeal, flour, salt and pepper in shallow bowl.
3. Heat oil in medium skillet over medium heat. Pat oysters dry with paper towels. Dip oysters in cornmeal mixture to coat. Fry in batches 5 minutes or until golden brown, turning once. Drain on paper towels.
4. Spread rolls with Spicy Mayonnaise; fill with lettuce, tomatoes and oysters.

spicy mayonnaise

Makes about ½ cup

½ cup mayonnaise
2 tablespoons plain yogurt
1 clove garlic, minced
¼ teaspoon ground red pepper

Combine mayonnaise, yogurt, garlic and red pepper in small bowl; mix until well blended. Refrigerate until ready to serve.

cajun blackened tuna

Makes 4 servings

  2 tablespoons butter, melted
  4 fresh tuna steaks, 1 inch thick (6 ounces each)
1½ teaspoons garlic salt
  1 teaspoon paprika
  1 teaspoon dried thyme or oregano
½ teaspoon ground cumin
¼ teaspoon ground red pepper
⅛ teaspoon white pepper
⅛ teaspoon black pepper
  4 lemon wedges (optional)

1. Prepare grill for direct cooking. Brush butter over both sides of tuna. Combine garlic salt, paprika, thyme, cumin, red pepper, white pepper and black pepper in small bowl; mix well. Sprinkle over both sides of tuna.

2. Place tuna on grid over medium-high heat. Grill 2 to 3 minutes per side for medium-rare. Serve with lemon wedges, if desired.

> **Tip:** Well done tuna steaks become tough and lose flavor. A good tuna steak is browned on both sides, but still pink in the center.

93 - Fish 'n Seafood

cajun blackened tuna

hoppin' shrimp and brown rice

Makes 4 servings

1 bag boil-in-bag instant brown rice
Nonstick cooking spray
2 cups frozen black-eyed peas
2 cups vegetable broth
2 cups salsa with jalapeños
1 can (about 14 ounces) diced tomatoes
1 bag (12 ounces) cooked baby shrimp
1 package (10 ounces) frozen whole okra
4 stalks celery, chopped
¼ cup chopped red onion
¼ cup chopped fresh cilantro
Juice of ½ lime
½ teaspoon black pepper
Lime wedges and fresh cilantro sprigs (optional)

1. Prepare rice according to package directions.

2. Spray large skillet with cooking spray; add black-eyed peas, broth, salsa, tomatoes, shrimp, okra, celery, onion, chopped cilantro, lime juice and black pepper. Simmer over medium-high heat 20 minutes or until heated through, stirring occasionally.

3. Top shrimp mixture with rice. Garnish with lime wedges and cilantro sprigs.

hoppin' shrimp and brown rice

southern fried catfish with hush puppies

Makes 4 servings

4 catfish fillets (about 1½ pounds)
½ cup yellow cornmeal
3 tablespoons all-purpose flour
1½ teaspoons salt
¼ teaspoon ground red pepper
Vegetable oil for frying
Hush Puppies (recipe follows)

1. Rinse catfish; pat dry with paper towels. Combine cornmeal, flour, salt and red pepper in shallow dish. Dip fish into cornmeal mixture.

2. Heat 1 inch oil in large heavy skillet over medium heat until 375°F on deep-fry thermometer. Cook fish in batches 4 to 5 minutes or until golden brown and fish begins to flake when tested with fork. Drain fish on paper towels; keep warm. *Allow temperature of oil to return to 375°F between batches.*

3. Prepare Hush Puppies. Serve with fish.

hush puppies

Makes about 24 hush puppies

1½ cups yellow cornmeal
½ cup all-purpose flour
2 teaspoons baking powder
½ teaspoon salt
1 cup milk
1 small onion, minced
1 egg, lightly beaten

1. Combine cornmeal, flour, baking powder and salt in medium bowl. Add milk, onion and egg; stir until well blended. Allow batter to stand 5 to 10 minutes.

2. Drop batter by tablespoonfuls into hot oil in batches. Cook 2 minutes or until golden brown. Drain on paper towels.

southern fried catfish with hush puppies

shrimp and garlic-parmesan grits

Makes 4 servings

2¼ cups water
½ cup quick-cooking grits
1 teaspoon dried oregano
½ teaspoon smoked paprika
½ teaspoon dried basil
½ teaspoon salt, divided
¼ to ½ teaspoon black pepper
⅛ to ¼ teaspoon ground red pepper (optional)
1 tablespoon olive oil
8 ounces medium raw shrimp, peeled
¾ cup chopped green onions
2 tablespoons milk
2 tablespoons butter
¼ teaspoon garlic powder
¼ cup grated Parmesan cheese
Lemon wedges (optional)

1. Bring water to a boil in medium saucepan over high heat; gradually stir in grits. Reduce heat; cover and simmer 9 minutes or until thickened, stirring occasionally. Set aside and keep warm.

2. Meanwhile, combine oregano, paprika, basil, ¼ teaspoon salt, black pepper and red pepper, if desired, in small bowl. Heat oil in large nonstick skillet over medium-high heat; add shrimp. Sprinkle with oregano mixture; cook 4 minutes or until shrimp are pink and opaque, stirring frequently. Remove from heat. Stir in green onions.

3. Whisk milk, butter, garlic powder and remaining ¼ teaspoon salt into grits. Sprinkle grits with cheese and top with shrimp mixture. Serve with lemon wedges, if desired.

99 - Fish 'n Seafood

shrimp and garlic-parmesan grits

baked halibut creole

Makes 4 servings

4 fresh or thawed frozen halibut steaks, 1 inch thick (about 1½ pounds)
Salt and black pepper
1 can (8 ounces) tomato sauce
1 package (12 ounces) frozen mixed vegetables such as broccoli, peas, onions and bell peppers
Hot cooked rice

1. Preheat oven to 350°F. Rinse halibut and pat dry with paper towels. Place in 13×9-inch baking pan. Season with salt and pepper.

2. Top fish with tomato sauce and mixed vegetables; season with salt and pepper.

3. Bake 25 to 30 minutes or until fish begins to flake when tested with fork. Serve over rice.

magic fried oysters

Makes 6 servings

6 dozen medium to large shucked oysters in their liquor (about 3 pounds)
3 tablespoons Chef Paul Prudhomme's Seafood Magic®
1 cup all-purpose flour
1 cup corn flour
1 cup cornmeal
Vegetable oil for deep-frying

Place oysters and oyster liquor in large bowl. Add 2 tablespoons of the Seafood Magic® to oysters, stirring well. In medium bowl, combine flour, corn flour, cornmeal and the remaining 1 tablespoon Seafood Magic®. Heat 2 inches or more of oil in deep-fryer or large saucepan to 375°F. Drain oysters and then use a slotted spoon to toss them lightly and quickly in seasoned flour mixture (so oysters don't produce excess moisture, which cakes the flour); shake off excess flour and carefully slip each oyster into hot oil. Fry in single layer in batches just until crispy and golden brown, 1 to 1½ minutes; do not overcook. (Adjust heat as needed to maintain temperature at about 375°F.) Drain on paper towels and serve.

101 - Fish 'n Seafood

baked halibut creole

blackened catfish with easy tartar sauce and rice

Makes 4 servings

    Easy Tartar Sauce (recipe follows)
- 4 catfish fillets (4 ounces each)
- 2 teaspoons lemon juice
- Nonstick garlic-flavored cooking spray
- 2 teaspoons blackened or Cajun seasoning
- 1 cup hot cooked rice

1. Prepare Easy Tartar Sauce.

2. Rinse catfish and pat dry with paper towels. Sprinkle with lemon juice; coat with cooking spray. Sprinkle with blackened seasoning; coat again with cooking spray.

3. Heat large nonstick skillet over medium-high heat. Add 2 fillets to skillet, seasoned side down; cook 3 minutes per side. Reduce heat to medium; cook 3 minutes or until fish begins to flake when tested with fork. Remove fillets from skillet; keep warm. Repeat with remaining fillets. Serve with Easy Tartar Sauce and rice.

easy tartar sauce

Makes about ¼ cup

- ¼ cup mayonnaise
- 2 tablespoons sweet pickle relish
- 1 teaspoon lemon juice

Combine mayonnaise, relish and lemon juice in small bowl; mix well. Refrigerate until ready to serve.

blackened catfish with easy tartar sauce and rice

black-eyed pea and chicken salad

Makes 4 servings

2½ cups chopped cooked chicken
1 can (about 15 ounces) black-eyed peas, rinsed and drained, or 1½ cups fresh or frozen, cooked and drained
1 cup chopped celery
1 cup chopped green and yellow bell peppers
½ cup chopped red onion
¼ cup mayonnaise
¼ cup plain yogurt
1 pickled jalapeño pepper,* drained, seeded and minced
1 teaspoon pickled jalapeño juice
¼ to ½ teaspoon salt
2 red bell peppers, halved and seeded
Chopped fresh parsley (optional)

*Jalapeño peppers can sting and irritate the skin, so wear rubber gloves when handling peppers and do not touch your eyes.

1. Combine chicken, black-eyed peas, celery, chopped green and yellow bell peppers and onion in large bowl; mix gently. Combine mayonnaise, yogurt, jalapeño pepper, jalapeño juice and salt in small bowl; blend well.

2. Toss mayonnaise mixture with chicken mixture. Spoon salad mixture evenly into centers of red bell pepper halves. Garnish with parsley.

Note: A black-eyed pea is really a bean, not a pea. Black-eyed peas are small, tan beans that take their name from the black eye-shaped mark on the inner curve of the bean.

107 - Sides 'n Salads

black-eyed pea and chicken salad

grilled cajun potato wedges

Makes 4 to 6 servings

3 large unpeeled russet potatoes, scrubbed (about 2¼ pounds)
¼ cup olive oil
2 cloves garlic, minced
1 teaspoon salt
1 teaspoon paprika
½ teaspoon dried thyme
½ teaspoon dried oregano
¼ teaspoon black pepper
⅛ to ¼ teaspoon ground red pepper
2 cups mesquite chips

1. Prepare grill for direct cooking. Preheat oven to 425°F.

2. Cut potatoes in half lengthwise, then cut each half lengthwise into 4 wedges. Place potatoes in large bowl. Add oil and garlic; toss to coat well.

3. Combine salt, paprika, thyme, oregano, black pepper and ground red pepper in small bowl. Sprinkle over potatoes; toss to coat well. Place potato wedges in single layer in shallow roasting pan. (Reserve remaining oil mixture left in large bowl.) Bake 20 minutes.

4. Meanwhile, cover mesquite chips with cold water; soak 20 minutes. Drain mesquite chips; sprinkle over coals. Place potato wedges on grid. Grill potato wedges, covered, over medium coals 15 to 20 minutes or until potatoes are browned and fork-tender. Brush with reserved oil mixture halfway through grilling time, turning once.

cajun dirty rice

Makes 6 servings

½ pound pork sausage, crumbled
1 small onion, finely chopped
1 stalk celery, finely chopped
1 small clove garlic, minced
2 cups chicken broth
1 tablespoon Cajun seasoning
2 cups MINUTE® White Rice, uncooked

Cook sausage in medium skillet over medium heat until evenly browned, stirring occasionally.

Add onions, celery and garlic; cook and stir 5 minutes or until sausage is cooked through and vegetables are tender.

Add broth to skillet with seasoning; stir. Bring to a boil. Stir in rice; cover. Remove from heat. Let stand 5 minutes. Fluff with fork.

Variation: For a more authentic dish, reduce sausage to ¼ pound and add ¼ pound chopped chicken livers.

bacon-cheese grits

Makes 4 servings

2 cups milk
½ cup quick-cooking grits
1½ cups (6 ounces) shredded sharp Cheddar cheese *or* 6 slices American cheese, torn into bite-size pieces
2 tablespoons butter
1 teaspoon Worcestershire sauce
½ teaspoon salt
⅛ teaspoon ground red pepper (optional)
4 thick-cut slices bacon, crisp-cooked and chopped

1. Bring milk to a boil in large saucepan over medium-high heat; slowly stir in grits. Return to a boil. Reduce heat. Cover; simmer 5 minutes, stirring frequently.

2. Remove grits from heat. Stir in cheese, butter, Worcestershire sauce, salt and red pepper, if desired. Cover; let stand 2 minutes or until cheese is melted. Top each serving with bacon.

country-style corn

Makes 6 to 8 servings

4 slices bacon
1 tablespoon all-purpose flour
1 can (about 15 ounces) corn, drained
1 can (about 15 ounces) cream-style corn
1 red bell pepper, diced
½ cup sliced green onions
Salt and black pepper

1. Cook bacon in large skillet over medium heat until crisp; drain on paper towels. Crumble bacon; set aside.

2. Whisk flour into drippings in skillet. Add corn, cream-style corn and bell pepper; bring to a boil. Reduce heat to low. Cook 10 minutes or until thickened.

3. Stir green onions and bacon into corn mixture. Season with salt and black pepper.

111 - Sides 'n Salads

bacon-cheese grits

carrot raisin salad

Makes 4 servings

2 to 3 carrots, shredded (1½ cups)
¼ cup raisins
¼ cup canned crushed pineapple, drained
1 tablespoon plain yogurt
4 lettuce leaves (optional)

1. Combine carrots, raisins, pineapple and yogurt in large bowl.

2. Refrigerate 2 hours; stir occasionally. Serve on lettuce leaves, if desired.

bayou dirty rice

Makes 4 to 6 servings

¼ pound spicy sausage, crumbled
½ medium onion, chopped
1 stalk celery, sliced
1 package (6 ounces) wild and long grain rice seasoned mix
1 can (14½ ounces) DEL MONTE® Original Recipe Stewed Tomatoes
½ green bell pepper, chopped
¼ cup chopped fresh parsley

1. Brown sausage and onion in large skillet over medium-high heat; drain. Add celery, rice and rice seasoning packet; cook and stir 2 minutes.

2. Drain tomatoes, reserving liquid; pour liquid into measuring cup. Add water to measure 1⅓ cups; pour over rice. Add tomatoes; bring to a boil. Cover and cook over low heat 20 minutes. Add bell pepper and parsley.

3. Cover and cook 5 minutes or until rice is tender. Serve with roasted chicken or Cornish game hens.

Prep and Cook Time: 40 minutes

carrot raisin salad

southern pecan cornbread stuffing

Makes 8 servings

5 cups dry cornbread stuffing mix
1 package KNORR® Leek Recipe Mix
½ cup (1 stick) I CAN'T BELIEVE IT'S NOT BUTTER!® Spread
1 cup coarsely chopped pecans
1 package (10 ounces) frozen corn, thawed and drained
1 cup hot water
1 cup orange juice

1. Preheat oven to 350°F. In large bowl, combine stuffing and recipe mix.

2. In 8-inch skillet, melt I Can't Believe It's Not Butter!® Spread over medium heat and cook pecans, stirring occasionally, 5 minutes.

3. Add corn, water, orange juice and pecan mixture to stuffing; toss until moistened. Spoon into 2-quart casserole sprayed with cooking spray.

4. Cover and bake 30 minutes or until heated through.

Prep Time: 5 minutes
Cook Time: 35 minutes

garlicky mustard greens

Makes 4 servings

2 pounds mustard greens
1 teaspoon olive oil
1 cup chopped onion
2 cloves garlic, minced
¾ cup chopped red bell pepper
½ cup chicken or vegetable broth
1 tablespoon cider vinegar
1 teaspoon sugar

1. Remove stems and any wilted leaves from greens. Stack several leaves; roll up. Cut crosswise into 1-inch slices. Repeat with remaining greens.

2. Heat oil in large saucepan over medium heat. Add onion and garlic; cook and stir 5 minutes or until onion is tender. Stir in greens, bell pepper and broth. Reduce heat to low. Cover and cook 25 minutes or until greens are tender, stirring occasionally.

3. Combine vinegar and sugar in small bowl; stir until sugar is dissolved. Stir into cooked greens. Serve immediately.

barbecue ranch chicken salad

Makes 4 servings

    Thick Barbecue Sauce (page 172), divided
  2 chicken breasts, grilled and cut into strips
  1 package mixed salad greens
  1 tomato, cut into wedges
  ½ cup thinly sliced red onion
  ½ cup canned corn, rinsed and drained
  ½ cup canned black beans, rinsed and drained
  ½ cup ranch salad dressing
  ½ cup (2 ounces) shredded Cheddar cheese

1. Prepare Thick Barbecue Sauce. Toss chicken lightly with ½ cup sauce.

2. Mix salad greens, tomato, onion, corn and beans in medium bowl.

3. Top salad with chicken. Drizzle with ranch dressing and sprinkle with cheese. Serve with additional Thick Barbecue Sauce, if desired.

creole red bean and rice salad

Makes 4 servings

1 cup dried red beans, sorted and rinsed
Salt
6 sun-dried tomatoes (not packed in oil), chopped
1 cup water
½ cup uncooked basmati or Texmati rice
Creole Dressing (page 176)
1 medium yellow squash, cut into ½-inch cubes
¾ cup finely diced red bell pepper
¾ cup finely diced celery
6 green onions, cut into ¼-inch slices

1. Place beans in large saucepan; cover with water by 2 inches. Bring to a boil over high heat. Cover and remove from heat. Let stand 1 hour. Return to a boil over high heat. Reduce heat to low. Cover and simmer 30 minutes. Season with salt; cook 15 to 30 minutes or until tender, adding tomatoes during last 5 minutes of cooking time.

2. Meanwhile, bring 1 cup water to a boil in medium saucepan. Add rice and season with salt. Reduce heat to low. Cover and simmer 25 to 30 minutes or until liquid is absorbed and rice is tender. Cool.

3. Meanwhile, prepare Creole Dressing. Set aside.

4. Drain bean mixture and rinse under cold water; drain. Place bean mixture, rice, squash, bell pepper, celery and green onions in large bowl. Pour Creole Dressing over bean mixture; toss to coat.

Tip: Dried beans have a firmer texture and fresher flavor than canned beans. They will keep up to a year in your pantry.

creole red bean and rice salad

grilled corn on the cob with buttery citrus spread

Makes 4 servings

- 4 medium ears corn, husks and silks removed
- Nonstick cooking spray
- 2 tablespoons butter
- 1 tablespoon finely chopped fresh parsley
- 1 teaspoon grated lemon peel
- ¼ teaspoon paprika
- Salt and black pepper

1. Prepare grill for direct cooking. Coat corn with nonstick cooking spray. Grill corn, covered, over medium heat 18 to 20 minutes or until golden brown, turning frequently.

2. Meanwhile, combine butter, parsley, lemon peel, paprika, salt and pepper in small bowl. Serve with corn.

glazed maple acorn squash

Makes 4 servings

- 1 large acorn or golden acorn squash
- ¼ cup water
- 2 tablespoons pure maple syrup
- 1 tablespoon butter, melted
- ¼ teaspoon ground cinnamon

1. Preheat oven to 375°F.

2. Cut stem and blossom ends from squash. Cut squash crosswise into 4 equal slices. Discard seeds and membrane. Place water in 13×9-inch baking dish. Arrange squash in dish; cover with foil. Bake 30 minutes or until tender.

3. Combine maple syrup, butter and cinnamon in small bowl; mix well. Uncover squash; pour off water. Brush squash with syrup mixture, letting excess pool in center of squash rings.

4. Bake 10 minutes or until syrup mixture is bubbly.

119 - Sides 'n Salads

grilled corn on the cob with buttery citrus spread

southern-style succotash

Makes 6 servings

  2 tablespoons butter
  1 cup chopped onion
  1 package (10 ounces) frozen lima beans, thawed
  1 cup frozen corn, thawed
  ½ cup chopped red bell pepper
  1 can (about 15 ounces) hominy, rinsed and drained
  ⅓ cup chicken broth
  ½ teaspoon salt
  ¼ teaspoon hot pepper sauce
  ¼ cup chopped green onion tops or fresh chives

1. Melt butter in large nonstick skillet over medium heat. Add onion; cook and stir 5 minutes. Add lima beans, corn and bell pepper; cook and stir 5 minutes.

2. Add hominy, broth, salt and hot pepper sauce; simmer 5 minutes or until most liquid is evaporated. Remove from heat. Stir in green onions before serving.

apricot coleslaw

Makes 4 to 6 servings

  ¼ cup balsamic vinegar
  2 tablespoons extra-virgin olive oil
  ¼ cup apricot preserves
  ¼ cup chopped fresh basil
  ½ teaspoon minced garlic
  ¼ teaspoon black pepper
  3 cups shredded cabbage or coleslaw mix

Combine vinegar, oil, preserves, basil, garlic and black pepper in large bowl; stir until blended. Toss with cabbage.

121 - Sides 'n Salads

southern-style succotash

sweet potato & pecan casserole

Makes 6 to 8 servings

1 can (40 ounces) sweet potatoes, drained and mashed
½ cup apple juice
⅓ cup plus 2 tablespoons butter, melted, divided
½ teaspoon salt
½ teaspoon ground cinnamon
¼ teaspoon black pepper
2 eggs, beaten
⅓ cup chopped pecans
⅓ cup packed brown sugar
2 tablespoons all-purpose flour

Slow Cooker Directions

1. Lightly grease slow cooker. Combine sweet potatoes, apple juice, ⅓ cup butter, salt, cinnamon and pepper in large bowl. Beat in eggs. Place mixture into prepared slow cooker.

2. Combine pecans, brown sugar, flour and remaining 2 tablespoons butter in small bowl. Spread over sweet potatoes. Cover; cook on HIGH 3 to 4 hours.

red beans & rice

Makes 6 servings

2 cans (about 15 ounces each) red beans, undrained
1 can (about 14 ounces) diced tomatoes
½ cup chopped celery
½ cup chopped green bell pepper
½ cup chopped green onions
2 cloves garlic, minced
1 to 2 teaspoons hot pepper sauce
1 teaspoon Worcestershire sauce
1 bay leaf
3 cups hot cooked rice

Slow Cooker Directions

1. Combine beans, tomatoes, celery, bell pepper, green onions, garlic, hot pepper sauce, Worcestershire sauce and bay leaf in slow cooker. Cover; cook on LOW 4 to 6 hours or on HIGH 2 to 3 hours.

2. Mash mixture slightly in slow cooker with potato masher until mixture thickens. *Increase temperature to HIGH.* Cook on HIGH 30 to 60 minutes. Remove and discard bay leaf. Serve bean mixture over rice.

corn and black-eyed pea salad

Makes 8 servings

 1 bag (16 ounces) frozen whole kernel corn, thawed (about 3 cups)
 1 can (about 15 ounces) black-eyed peas, rinsed and drained
 1 large green pepper, chopped (about 1 cup)
 1 medium onion, chopped (about ½ cup)
 ½ cup chopped fresh cilantro leaves
 1 jar (16 ounces) PACE® Picante Sauce

1. Stir the corn, peas, green pepper, onion and cilantro in a medium bowl. Add the picante sauce and stir to coat.

2. Cover and refrigerate for 4 hours. Stir before serving.

Prep Time: 15 minutes
Cook Time: 4 hours
Total Time: 4 hours 15 minutes

Cakes 'n Pies

southern oatmeal pie

Makes 8 servings

½ (about 15-ounce) package refrigerated pie crusts
4 eggs
1 cup light corn syrup
½ cup packed brown sugar
¼ cup (½ stick) plus 2 tablespoons unsalted butter, melted and slightly cooled
1½ teaspoons vanilla
½ teaspoon salt
1 cup quick oats
Whipped cream and sliced plums (optional)

1. Preheat oven to 375°F. Let crust stand at room temperature 15 minutes. Line 9-inch pie plate with crust; flute edge.

2. Whisk eggs in medium bowl. Whisk in corn syrup, brown sugar, butter, vanilla and salt until well blended. Stir in oats. Pour into crust.

3. Bake 35 minutes or until edge is set. Cool on wire rack. Serve with whipped cream and plums, if desired.

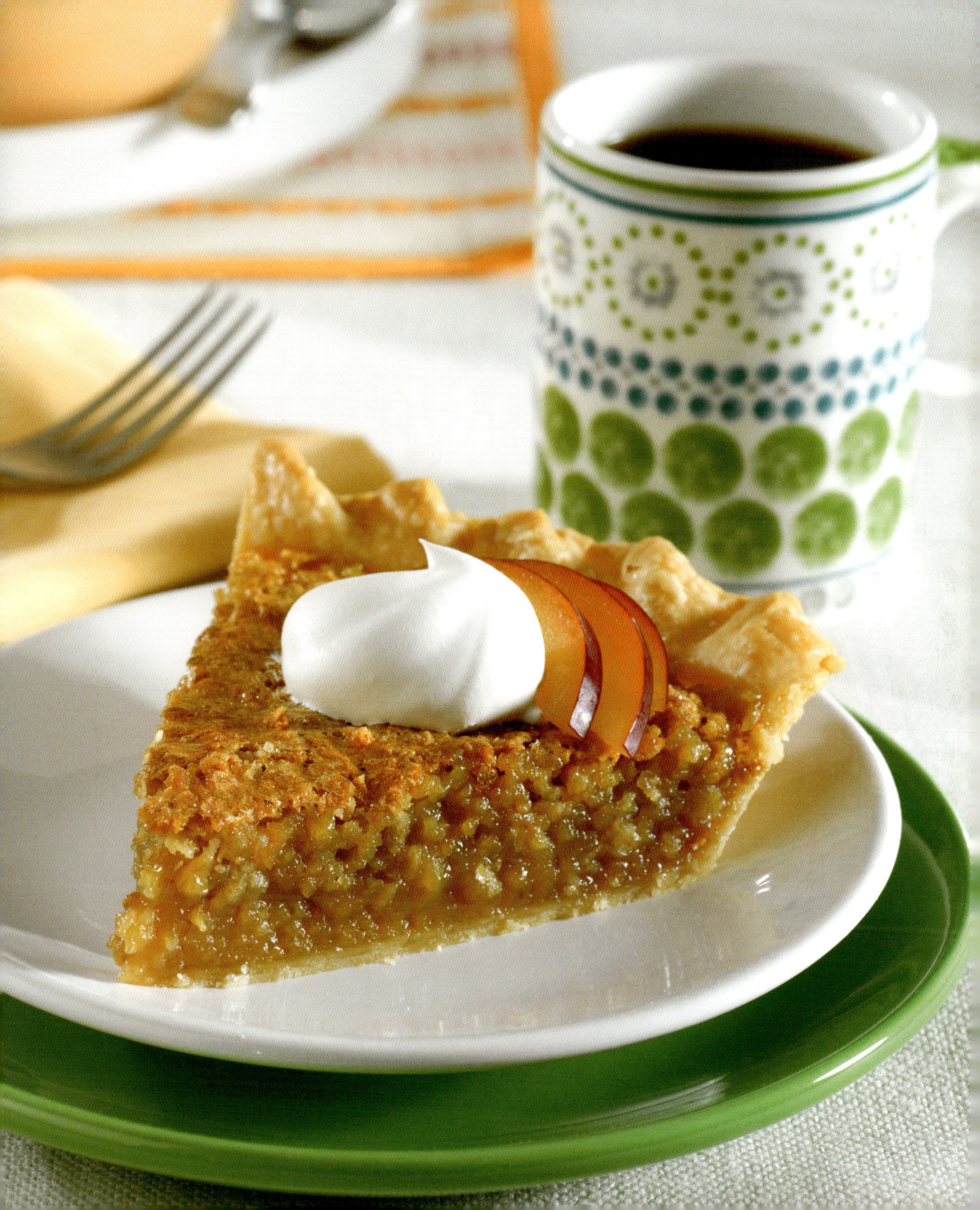

banana praline ice cream cake

Makes 12 servings

   3 ripe medium bananas,* divided
   1 package (about 18 ounces) German chocolate cake mix
1⅓ cups water
   3 eggs
 ⅓ cup vegetable oil
   2 cups chopped pecans
 ½ cup (1 stick) butter
 ½ cup packed dark brown sugar
   2 teaspoons ground cinnamon
   2 cups vanilla ice cream, slightly softened
 ¼ cup caramel ice cream topping

*Do not use overripe bananas.

1. Preheat oven to 325°F. Line two 8-inch round cake pans with parchment paper.

2. Mash 2 bananas with fork. Combine mashed bananas, cake mix, water, eggs and oil in large bowl; beat according to package directions. Divide batter evenly between prepared pans.

3. Bake 33 to 35 minutes or until toothpick inserted into centers comes out clean. Cool in pans on wire rack 15 minutes. Invert onto wire rack to cool completely. (For easier cake assembly, wrap layers in plastic wrap and freeze overnight.)

4. Heat large nonstick skillet over medium-high heat. Add pecans; cook and stir 2 minutes or until pecans begin to lightly brown. Add butter, brown sugar and cinnamon; cook and stir until butter is melted. Remove from heat; cool completely. Reserve ½ cup praline pecans; set aside.

5. Slice remaining banana. Place one cake layer on serving platter. Working quickly, spoon ice cream evenly over cake. Sprinkle evenly with 1½ cups praline pecans. Place remaining cake layer on top. Spread caramel topping evenly on top layer. Arrange banana slices on caramel topping; sprinkle evenly with reserved ½ cup praline pecans. Freeze overnight or until firm. Allow cake to stand a few minutes before slicing.

Tip: Prepare the ice cream layer in advance. Line an 8-inch round cake pan with plastic wrap. Fill the pan with ice cream. Freeze 1 to 2 hours or until firm. Using the plastic wrap, pop the ice cream layer out of the pan. If you need the pan for baking, place the wrapped ice cream round in the freezer until you are ready to assemble the cake.

127 - Cakes 'n Pies

banana praline ice cream cake

shoo fly pie

Makes 8 servings

- 1 cup all-purpose flour
- ⅔ cup packed brown sugar
- ¼ cup (½ stick) plus 1 tablespoon unsalted butter, cubed, divided
- 3 eggs, beaten
- ½ cup molasses
- ½ teaspoon baking soda
- ⅔ cup hot water
- 1 unbaked deep-dish 9-inch pie crust
- Whipped cream (optional)

1. Preheat oven to 325°F.

2. Combine flour and brown sugar in medium bowl. For topping, transfer ½ cup flour mixture to small bowl. Cut in 1 tablespoon butter with pastry blender or two knives until mixture resembles coarse crumbs.

3. Melt remaining ¼ cup butter in small heavy saucepan over low heat; cool slightly. Combine eggs, molasses and melted butter in large bowl. Gradually stir in remaining flour mixture and baking soda until well blended. Stir in water until blended. Pour into crust. Sprinkle with topping.

4. Bake 40 minutes or until filling is puffy and set. Cool completely on wire rack. Serve with whipped cream, if desired.

shoo fly pie

sweet potato pie

Makes 8 servings

3 large sweet potatoes, peeled and cut into cubes (about 3 cups)
¼ cup heavy cream
1 can (10¾ ounces) CAMPBELL'S® Condensed Tomato Soup
1 cup packed brown sugar
3 eggs
1 teaspoon vanilla extract
½ teaspoon ground cinnamon
½ teaspoon ground nutmeg
1 (9-inch) frozen pie crust

1. Heat the oven to 350°F.

2. Place potatoes into a 3-quart saucepan and add water to cover. Heat over medium-high heat to a boil. Reduce the heat to low. Cover and cook for 10 minutes or until the potatoes are tender. Drain the potatoes well in a colander.

3. Place the potatoes and heavy cream into a large bowl. Beat with an electric mixer on medium speed until the mixture is fluffy. Beat in the soup, brown sugar, eggs, vanilla extract, cinnamon and nutmeg. Pour the potato mixture into the pie crust and place onto a baking sheet.

4. Bake for 1 hour or until set. Cool the pie in the pan on a wire rack about 3 hours.

Kitchen Tip: Substitute 1¾ cups drained and mashed canned sweet potatoes for the fresh mashed sweet potatoes.

Prep Time: 15 minutes
Bake Time: 1 hour
Cool Time: 3 hours

turtle pecan pie

Makes 8 servings

1 frozen deep-dish 9-inch pie crust
1 cup light corn syrup
3 eggs, lightly beaten
½ cup sugar
⅓ cup butter, melted
1 teaspoon vanilla
½ teaspoon salt
1 cup toasted pecans*
2 squares (1 ounce each) semisweet chocolate, melted
½ cup caramel ice cream topping
Whipped cream and grated chocolate (optional)

To toast pecans, spread in single layer on baking sheet. Bake in 350°F oven 8 to 10 minutes or until fragrant, stirring frequently.

1. Preheat oven to 350°F. Place frozen pie crust on baking sheet.

2. Combine corn syrup, eggs, sugar, butter, vanilla and salt in large bowl; mix well. Reserve ½ cup egg mixture. Stir pecans and chocolate into remaining egg mixture; pour into pie crust. Stir caramel topping into reserved egg mixture; carefully pour over pecan filling.

3. Bake 50 to 55 minutes or until filling is set about 3 inches from edge. Cool completely on wire rack. Garnish with whipped cream and grated chocolate.

pecan praline brandy cake

Makes 12 servings

- 1 package (about 18 ounces) butter pecan cake mix
- ¾ cup water
- ⅓ cup plain yogurt
- 2 egg whites
- 1 egg
- ¼ cup plus ½ teaspoon brandy, divided
- 2 tablespoons vegetable oil
- 1 cup chopped toasted pecans,* divided
- ⅔ cup packed light brown sugar
- ⅓ cup light corn syrup
- ¼ cup whipping cream
- 2 tablespoons butter
- ½ teaspoon vanilla

*To toast pecans, spread in single layer on baking sheet. Bake in 350°F oven 8 to 10 minutes or until fragrant, stirring frequently.

1. Preheat oven to 350°F. Spray 10- or 12-cup bundt pan with nonstick cooking spray.

2. Beat cake mix, water, yogurt, egg whites, egg, ¼ cup brandy and oil in medium bowl with electric mixer at low speed 30 seconds. Beat at medium speed 2 minutes or until light and fluffy. Fold in ½ cup pecans. Pour batter into prepared pan.

3. Bake 50 minutes or until toothpick inserted near center comes out clean. Cool in pan 10 minutes. Remove to wire rack; cool completely.

4. Combine brown sugar, corn syrup, cream and butter in small saucepan; bring to a boil over medium heat, stirring constantly. Remove from heat; stir in remaining ½ cup pecans, ½ teaspoon brandy and vanilla. Cool to room temperature. Pour over cake; let stand until set.

133 - CAKES 'N PIES

pecan praline brandy cake

black bottom pie

Makes 8 servings

- 1 envelope (¼ ounce) unflavored gelatin
- ¼ cup cold water
- ⅔ cup semisweet chocolate chips
- ½ cup granulated sugar
- 1 tablespoon cornstarch
- ¼ teaspoon salt
- 3 cups whipping cream, divided
- 3 eggs
- 1 (6-ounce) chocolate graham cracker pie crust
- 1 to 2 tablespoons rum
- 3 tablespoons powdered sugar
- Grated chocolate (optional)

1. Sprinkle gelatin over ¼ cup cold water in cup; let stand until ready to use. Place chocolate chips in medium bowl; set aside.

2. Combine granulated sugar, cornstarch and salt in medium heavy saucepan. Gradually add 1½ cups cream in steady stream, stirring constantly. Stir in eggs until well blended; cook over low heat 10 to 12 minutes or until thickened, stirring constantly.

3. Pour half of hot custard over chocolate chips; let stand 1 minute. Stir until chocolate is melted and mixture is smooth. Pour into crust; refrigerate.

4. Stir gelatin mixture into remaining custard about 30 seconds. Stir in ¾ cup cream and rum; refrigerate 45 to 60 minutes or until thickened but not set.

5. Beat rum custard in medium bowl with electric mixer at high speed 5 minutes or until smooth and fluffy; spread over chocolate layer.

6. Beat remaining ¾ cup cream and powdered sugar in large bowl with electric mixer at high speed until stiff peaks form; spread over rum custard layer. Refrigerate at least 1 hour or until ready to serve. Garnish with grated chocolate.

Note: If chocolate graham cracker pie crust is unavailable, combine 1⅓ cups chocolate graham cracker crumbs with ¼ cup (½ stick) melted butter in small bowl. Press onto bottom and up side of 9-inch pie plate. Bake in preheated 350°F oven 10 minutes; cool completely on wire rack.

sweet coconut custard pie

Makes 8 servings

½ (about 15-ounce) package refrigerated pie crusts
1 cup sugar
4 eggs
¾ cup buttermilk
¼ cup (½ stick) butter, melted and cooled
1 tablespoon cornstarch
1 teaspoon vanilla
¼ teaspoon salt
1 cup shredded coconut

1. Preheat oven to 350°F. Let crust stand at room temperature 15 minutes. Line 9-inch pie plate with crust; flute edge.

2. Combine sugar, eggs, buttermilk, butter, cornstarch, vanilla and salt in large bowl; whisk until smooth. Stir in coconut. Pour mixture into crust.

3. Bake 45 minutes or until set. Cool completely on wire rack.

sweet potato crumb cake

Makes 6 cakes

½ cup granulated sugar
Grated peel of 1 orange
½ cup chopped pecans
1 teaspoon ground cinnamon
¼ cup all-purpose flour
¼ cup oats
¼ cup (½ stick) cold butter, cut into pieces
1 package (16 ounces) sweet potato pound cake mix, plus ingredients to prepare mix
Powdered sugar (optional)

1. Preheat oven to 350°F. Spray six individual loaf pans with nonstick cooking spray.*

2. Combine granulated sugar and orange peel in food processor; pulse using on/off action several times to thoroughly mix. Add pecans and cinnamon; pulse until pecans are size of peas. Reserve ⅓ cup crumb mixture; set aside.

3. Add flour, oats and butter to remaining crumb mixture in food processor; pulse until mixture resembles coarse crumbs.

4. Prepare cake mix according to package directions. Divide batter in half. Evenly pour one half into prepared pans. Evenly sprinkle with ⅓ cup reserved crumb mixture. Spoon remaining batter evenly over crumb mixture. Top with oat crumb mixture.

5. Bake 25 to 30 minutes or until toothpick inserted into centers comes out clean. Cool in pans 15 minutes. Remove to wire rack; cool completely. Dust with powdered sugar, if desired.

*Eight standard (2½-inch) muffin cups may be substituted.

sweet potato crumb cake

lemon chess pie

Makes 8 servings

½ (about 15-ounce) package refrigerated pie crusts
1¾ cups sugar
3 eggs
2 egg yolks
½ cup half-and-half
3 tablespoons grated lemon peel
⅓ cup lemon juice
¼ cup (½ stick) butter, melted
2 tablespoons all-purpose flour
Whipped cream (optional)
Lemon peel strips (optional)

1. Preheat oven to 325°F. Let crust stand at room temperature 15 minutes. Line 9-inch pie plate with crust; flute edge.

2. Whisk sugar, eggs, egg yolks, half-and-half, grated lemon peel, lemon juice, butter and flour in large bowl until well blended. Pour into crust.

3. Bake 40 minutes or until almost set. Cool completely on wire rack. Refrigerate 2 hours or until ready to serve. Serve with whipped cream, if desired. Garnish with lemon peel strips.

> **Tip:** To flute the edge of a pie crust, fold the overhang of the crust under and stand the edge up. Press your thumb on the inside of the crust gently into the thumb and index finger of your opposite hand on the outside of the crust to create a groove; continue evenly around the edge of the crust.

141 - Cakes 'n Pies

lemon chess pie

tropical bananas foster upside-down cake

◦♢ *Makes 12 servings* ♢◦

¼ cup (½ stick) butter
2 tablespoons rum *or* 1 teaspoon rum flavoring
½ cup packed brown sugar
2 large bananas, cut diagonally into ¼-inch pieces
1 package (about 18 ounces) banana walnut bread mix, plus ingredients to prepare mix
1 cup flaked coconut, plus additional for garnish
Vanilla ice cream (optional)

1. Preheat oven to 350°F. Line baking sheet with foil. Spray bottom and side of 9-inch springform pan with nonstick cooking spray. Place pan on baking sheet.

2. Melt butter in small saucepan over low heat. Add rum; cook and stir 2 minutes. Stir in brown sugar; remove from heat. Pour sugar mixture into prepared pan; swirl to coat bottom evenly. Arrange banana pieces in even layer on sugar mixture.

3. Prepare bread mix according to package directions. Stir in coconut. Pour batter over bananas.

4. Bake 45 minutes or until toothpick inserted into center comes out clean. Cool completely in pan on wire rack. Invert cake onto serving platter. Garnish with additional coconut and serve with vanilla ice cream, if desired.

143 - Cakes 'n Pies

tropical bananas foster upside-down cake

Mama's Desserts

peach turnovers

Makes 6 servings

- 2 cups chopped peeled fresh peaches or frozen unsweetened peach slices, thawed, drained and chopped
- 2 tablespoons granulated sugar
- 1 tablespoon all-purpose flour
- ¼ teaspoon vanilla
- ⅛ teaspoon ground nutmeg
- 6 sheets (about 12×8¼-inches each) frozen phyllo dough, thawed
- Nonstick cooking spray
- 1 tablespoon powdered sugar

1. Preheat oven to 375°F. Line baking sheet with parchment paper or foil. Combine peaches, granulated sugar, flour, vanilla and nutmeg in small bowl; toss until combined.

2. Place one sheet of phyllo dough on damp kitchen towel. (Keep remaining dough covered.) Lightly spray dough with cooking spray. Top with second sheet of phyllo. Using sharp knife or pizza cutter, cut into 2 lengthwise strips, each measuring about 12×4 inches.

3. For each turnover, spoon about ⅓ cup peach mixture onto dough about 1 inch from end of each strip. Fold one corner over filling to make triangle; continue folding turnover to form triangle that encloses filling. Repeat with remaining dough and filling. Place on prepared baking sheet. Lightly spray tops of turnovers with cooking spray.

4. Bake 17 minutes or until golden brown. Cool on wire rack 10 minutes. Sprinkle with powdered sugar. Serve immediately.

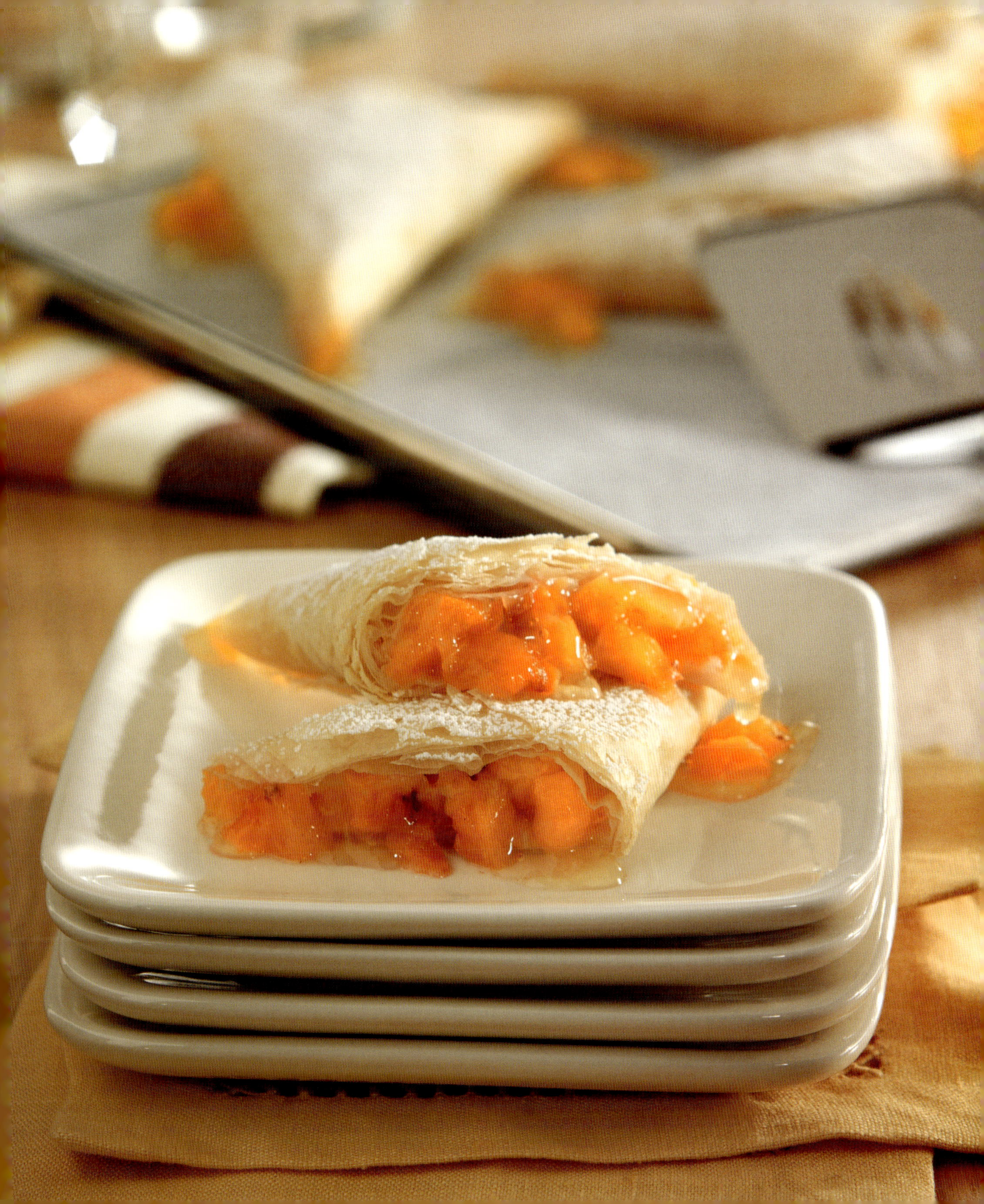

southern caramel apple bars

Makes about 2 dozen bars

  2 cups all-purpose flour
  1 teaspoon salt
  ½ teaspoon baking powder
  ½ teaspoon baking soda
  ⅔ cup butter
  ¾ cup packed light brown sugar
  ½ cup granulated sugar
  1 egg
  1 teaspoon vanilla
  4 Granny Smith apples, peeled and coarsely chopped
  ½ cup pecans, chopped
24 caramel candies, unwrapped
  2 tablespoons milk

1. Preheat oven to 350°F. Grease 13×9-inch baking dish.

2. Combine flour, salt, baking powder and baking soda in medium bowl. Melt butter in medium saucepan. Remove from heat; stir in brown sugar, granulated sugar, egg and vanilla until well blended. Add flour mixture; mix well. Press into bottom of prepared baking dish; top with apples.

3. Bake 40 to 45 minutes or until edges are browned and pulling away from sides of pan. Cool completely in pan on wire rack.

4. Toast pecans in medium nonstick skillet over medium-high heat 2 minutes or until fragrant, stirring constantly. Remove from skillet; set aside. Wipe out skillet with paper towel. Heat caramels and milk in same skillet over medium-low heat until melted and smooth, stirring constantly.

5. Drizzle caramel sauce over cooled apple bars; sprinkle with pecans. Let stand 30 minutes before cutting into bars.

southern caramel apple bars

steamed southern sweet potato custard

∽ Makes 4 servings ∽

1 can (16 ounces) cut sweet potatoes, drained
1 can (12 ounces) evaporated milk, divided
½ cup packed light brown sugar
2 eggs, lightly beaten
1 teaspoon ground cinnamon
½ teaspoon ground ginger
¼ teaspoon salt
Whipped cream and ground nutmeg (optional)

Slow Cooker Directions

1. Place sweet potatoes and ¼ cup evaporated milk in food processor or blender; process until smooth. Add remaining evaporated milk, brown sugar, eggs, cinnamon, ginger and salt; process until well blended. Pour into ungreased 1-quart soufflé dish. Cover tightly with foil. Crumple large sheet of foil (about 15×12 inches); place in bottom of slow cooker. Pour 2 cups water over foil. Make foil handles.*

2. Transfer dish to slow cooker using foil handles. Cover; cook on HIGH 2½ to 3 hours or until skewer inserted into center comes out clean.

3. Use foil handles to lift dish from slow cooker; transfer to wire rack. Uncover; let stand 30 minutes. Garnish with whipped cream and nutmeg.

*To make foil handles, tear off 3 (18×3-inch) strips of heavy-duty foil. Crisscross the strips so they resemble the spokes of a wheel. Place the dish in the center of the strips. Pull the foil strips up and over the dish and place it into the slow cooker. Leave the foil strips in while the custard cooks, so you can easily lift the dish out again when it is finished cooking.

149 - Mama's Desserts

steamed southern sweet potato custard

southern peanut butter cheesecake

Makes 10 servings

½ cup low-fat graham cracker crumbs
8 ounces cream cheese, softened and cut into cubes
8 ounces fat-free cream cheese, cut into cubes
½ cup fat-free sour cream
½ cup fat-free ricotta or low-fat cottage cheese
⅓ cup peanut butter
½ cup firmly packed dark brown sugar
2 teaspoons vanilla extract
6 egg whites *or* ¾ cup egg substitute

Coat a 9-inch springform pan with cooking spray. Sprinkle graham cracker crumbs evenly over the bottom of pan. Set aside. Process the cream cheese, sour cream and ricotta cheese in a food processor until smooth. Add the peanut butter and mix. Slowly add the sugar and vanilla extract. Slowly pour the eggs through the food chute with the processor running. Process until blended. Spoon the mixture over the graham cracker crumbs. Bake in a preheated 300°F oven for 50 minutes. Center will be soft, but will firm when chilled. Turn the oven off and leave the cheesecake in the oven for 30 minutes more. Remove from oven; let cool to room temperature on a wire rack. Cover and chill 8 hours. Garnish with chopped peanuts or serve with assorted fresh berries, if desired.

Favorite recipe from Peanut Advisory Board

peach cobbler

Makes 4 to 6 servings

2 packages (16 ounces each) frozen sliced peaches, thawed and drained
¾ cup plus 1 tablespoon sugar, divided
2 teaspoons ground cinnamon, divided
½ teaspoon ground nutmeg
¾ cup all-purpose flour
6 tablespoons butter, cut into pieces
Whipped cream (optional)

Slow Cooker Directions

1. Combine peaches, ¾ cup sugar, 1½ teaspoons cinnamon and nutmeg in medium bowl. Place into slow cooker.

2. For topping, combine flour, remaining 1 tablespoon sugar and ½ teaspoon cinnamon in small bowl. Cut in butter with pastry blender or two knives until mixture resembles coarse crumbs. Sprinkle over peach mixture. Cover; cook on HIGH 2 hours.

3. Serve with whipped cream, if desired.

fudge rum balls

Makes 6 dozen rum balls

1 package DUNCAN HINES® Moist Deluxe® Butter Recipe Fudge Cake Mix
2 cups sifted confectioners' sugar
1 cup finely chopped pecans or walnuts
¼ cup unsweetened cocoa powder
1 tablespoon rum extract
Pecans or walnuts, finely chopped

1. Preheat oven to 375°F. Grease and flour 13×9×2-inch pan.

2. Prepare, bake and cool cake following package directions for basic recipe.

3. Crumble cake into large bowl. Stir with fork until crumbs are fine and uniform in size. Add confectioners' sugar, 1 cup nuts, cocoa and rum extract. Stir until well blended.

4. Shape heaping tablespoonfuls of mixture into balls. Garnish by rolling balls in finely chopped nuts. Press firmly to adhere nuts.

Tip: You may substitute rum for the rum extract.

mississippi mud bars

Makes about 3 dozen triangles

¾ cup packed brown sugar
½ cup (1 stick) butter, softened
1 egg
1 teaspoon vanilla
1 cup plus 2 tablespoons all-purpose flour
½ teaspoon baking soda
¼ teaspoon salt
1 cup (6 ounces) semisweet chocolate chips, divided
1 cup (6 ounces) white chocolate chips, divided
½ cup chopped walnuts or pecans

1. Preheat oven to 375°F. Line 9-inch square baking pan with foil; grease foil.

2. Beat brown sugar and butter in large bowl with electric mixer at medium speed until well blended. Beat in egg and vanilla until blended. Blend in flour, baking soda and salt until well blended. Stir in ⅔ cup semisweet chips, ⅔ cup white chips and walnuts. Spread dough in prepared pan.

3. Bake 23 to 25 minutes or until center is firm to the touch. *Do not overbake.* Sprinkle with remaining ⅓ cup semisweet chips and ⅓ cup white chips. Let stand until chips soften; spread evenly over bars. Cool in pan on wire rack until chocolate is set. Cut into triangles.

153 - Mama's Desserts

mississippi mud bars

pecan bread pudding with caramel whiskey sauce

Makes 8 servings

    8 cups cubed egg bread or brioche (about 10 ounces)
    ½ cup coarsely chopped pecans, toasted*
  1⅔ cups sugar, divided
    3 eggs
    3 egg yolks
    3 cups whole milk
    1 teaspoon vanilla
    ¼ teaspoon salt
    ¼ teaspoon ground nutmeg
    1 teaspoon ground cinnamon
    2 tablespoons butter, cut into pieces
    ⅓ cup whipping cream
    2 to 3 tablespoons whiskey or bourbon

To toast pecans, spread in single layer on baking sheet. Bake in 350°F oven 8 to 10 minutes or until fragrant, stirring frequently.

1. Preheat oven to 350°F. Grease 13×9-inch baking dish or 2-quart shallow casserole. Place bread cubes and pecans in prepared baking dish.

2. Beat ¾ cup sugar, eggs and egg yolks in medium bowl with electric mixer at medium speed until blended. Add milk, vanilla, salt and nutmeg; beat until well blended. Pour egg mixture over bread mixture. Let stand 15 to 20 minutes, pressing down on bread occasionally. Combine ¼ cup sugar and cinnamon in small bowl; sprinkle over bread mixture.

3. Bake 45 to 50 minutes or until puffed and golden brown. Cool on wire rack 15 minutes before serving.

4. Place butter in heavy small saucepan. Add remaining ⅔ cup sugar; shake pan to make even layer but do not stir. Cook and stir over medium heat 5 minutes or until deep golden brown and bubbly. Gradually stir in cream; cook and stir until smooth. Remove from heat; stir in whiskey, 1 tablespoon at a time. Serve bread pudding with warm sauce.

155 - Mama's Desserts

pecan bread pudding with caramel whiskey sauce

fresh berry-berry cobbler

◈ *Makes 6 servings* ◈

¼ cup sugar
1 teaspoon cornstarch
12 ounces fresh raspberries
8 ounces fresh blueberries
¼ cup CREAM OF WHEAT® Hot Cereal (Instant, 1-minute, 2½-minute or 10-minute cook time), uncooked
¼ cup all-purpose flour
¼ cup ground almonds
2 teaspoons baking powder
¼ teaspoon salt
¼ cup (½ stick) butter, cut into small pieces, softened
¼ cup milk
1 egg
1 tablespoon sugar
Ice cream or whipped cream (optional)

1. Preheat oven to 450°F. Blend sugar and cornstarch in mixing bowl. Add berries and toss to coat. Pour into 8-inch square baking pan; set aside.

2. Combine Cream of Wheat, flour, almonds, baking powder and salt in food processor. Add butter; pulse several times until well combined. Add milk and egg; pulse until mixed thoroughly. Spread evenly over fruit mixture. Sprinkle sugar over top.

3. Bake 20 minutes. Let stand 5 minutes before serving. Serve in shallow bowls with ice cream or whipped cream, if desired.

Serving Suggestion: For an elegant presentation, serve in a martini glass and top with a fresh sprig of mint.

Prep Time: 10 minutes
Start to Finish Time: 35 minutes

157 - Mama's Desserts

fresh berry-berry cobbler

ambrosia

Makes 4 to 6 servings

1 can (20 ounces) DOLE® Pineapple Chunks, drained or 2 cups DOLE® Frozen Tropical Gold Pineapple Chunks, partially thawed
1 can (11 or 15 ounces) DOLE® Mandarin Oranges, drained
1 DOLE® Banana, sliced
1½ cups seedless grapes
½ cup miniature marshmallows
1 cup vanilla low fat yogurt
¼ cup flaked coconut, toasted

- Combine pineapple chunks, mandarin oranges, banana, grapes and marshmallows in medium bowl.

- Stir yogurt into fruit mixture. Sprinkle with coconut.

Prep Time: 15 minutes

extra chunky peanut butter cookies

Makes about 4 dozen cookies

2 cups all-purpose flour
1 teaspoon baking soda
½ teaspoon salt
1 cup chunky peanut butter
¾ cup granulated sugar
½ cup packed light brown sugar
½ cup (1 stick) butter, softened
2 eggs
1 teaspoon vanilla
1½ cups chopped chocolate-covered peanut butter cups (12 to 14 candies)
1 cup dry roasted peanuts

1. Preheat oven to 350°F. Line cookie sheets with parchment paper or lightly grease.

2. Combine flour, baking soda and salt in medium bowl. Beat peanut butter, granulated sugar, brown sugar and butter in large bowl with electric mixer at medium speed until creamy. Beat in eggs and vanilla. Add flour mixture; beat until well blended. Stir in candy and peanuts. Drop dough by rounded tablespoonfuls 2 inches apart onto prepared cookie sheets.

3. Bake 13 minutes or until set. Cool on cookie sheets 1 minute. Remove to wire racks; cool completely.

sweet and spicy bananas foster

Makes 4 servings

½ cup (1 stick) butter
½ cup firmly packed light brown sugar
2 tablespoons ORTEGA® Taco Seasoning Mix
4 bananas, peeled, halved and cut in half lengthwise
¼ cup dark rum
　Vanilla ice cream

Melt butter in large skillet over medium heat. Stir in brown sugar; cook and stir until smooth and sugar has dissolved. Stir in seasoning mix.

Add banana quarters; swirl around in skillet to coat bananas completely. Add rum; simmer 4 minutes or until alcohol has cooked out.

Place ice cream in serving dishes. Arrange 4 banana pieces in each dish; spoon sauce over ice cream and bananas.

Prep Time: 1 minute
Start to Finish: 5 minutes

Tip: For a warmer treat, serve this sweet and spicy version of Bananas Foster over pound cake or your favorite coffee cake.

benne wafers

Makes about 4 dozen wafers

6 tablespoons all-purpose flour
6 tablespoons whole wheat flour
¼ teaspoon salt
¼ teaspoon baking powder
½ cup (1 stick) unsalted butter, softened
½ cup packed light brown sugar
1 egg
½ teaspoon vanilla
½ cup sesame seeds, toasted*

*To toast sesame seeds, spread in single layer on baking sheet. Bake in 350°F oven 5 minutes or until lightly browned, stirring frequently. Transfer seeds to small bowl to cool.

1. Preheat oven to 350°F. Line two baking sheets with parchment paper.

2. Combine all-purpose flour, whole wheat flour, salt and baking powder in small bowl. Beat butter and brown sugar in medium bowl with electric mixer at high speed until light and fluffy. Beat in egg and vanilla. Gradually beat in flour mixture. Add sesame seeds; beat until well blended. Drop dough by rounded teaspoonfuls 2 inches apart onto prepared baking sheets. Flatten slightly with fork.

3. Bake 9 to 10 minutes or until lightly browned. Cool on baking sheets 5 minutes; transfer to wire racks to cool completely.

benne wafers

strawberry shortcake

Makes 6 servings

½ cup orange juice
1 tablespoon cornstarch
1 package (14 ounces) DOLE® Frozen Sliced Strawberries (2 cups), partially thawed
¼ cup sugar
1 tablespoon orange marmalade
6 prepared biscuits
Prepared sweetened whipped cream or aerosol whipped cream

- Stir orange juice into cornstarch in medium saucepan. Add strawberries, sugar and marmalade. Bring to a boil, stirring occasionally. Reduce heat to low; cook 2 minutes, stirring, or until sauce thickens. Cool or chill.

- Split open prepared biscuits. Spoon strawberry glaze over biscuits. Add spoonful whipped cream and biscuit top. Spoon additional glaze and strawberries over biscuits.

Prep Time: 10 minutes
Cook Time: 5 minutes

163 - Mama's Desserts

strawberry shortcake

Classic Condiments

cranberry-apple chutney

Makes 20 servings

- 1 cup chopped sweet onion
- 1 cup granulated sugar
- ¾ cup unsweetened apple juice
- ½ cup packed light brown sugar
- 1 teaspoon ground cinnamon
- ½ teaspoon ground ginger
- ⅛ teaspoon ground cloves
- 1 package (12 ounces) fresh or thawed frozen cranberries
- 1 large Granny Smith apple, peeled and cut into ½-inch pieces

1. Combine onion, granulated sugar, apple juice, brown sugar, cinnamon, ginger and cloves in medium heavy saucepan; bring to a boil over high heat. Reduce heat and simmer 5 minutes.

2. Add cranberries and apple; simmer 20 minutes or until mixture is very thick, stirring occasionally.

3. Cool to room temperature. Transfer to serving dish or refrigerate until ready to serve.

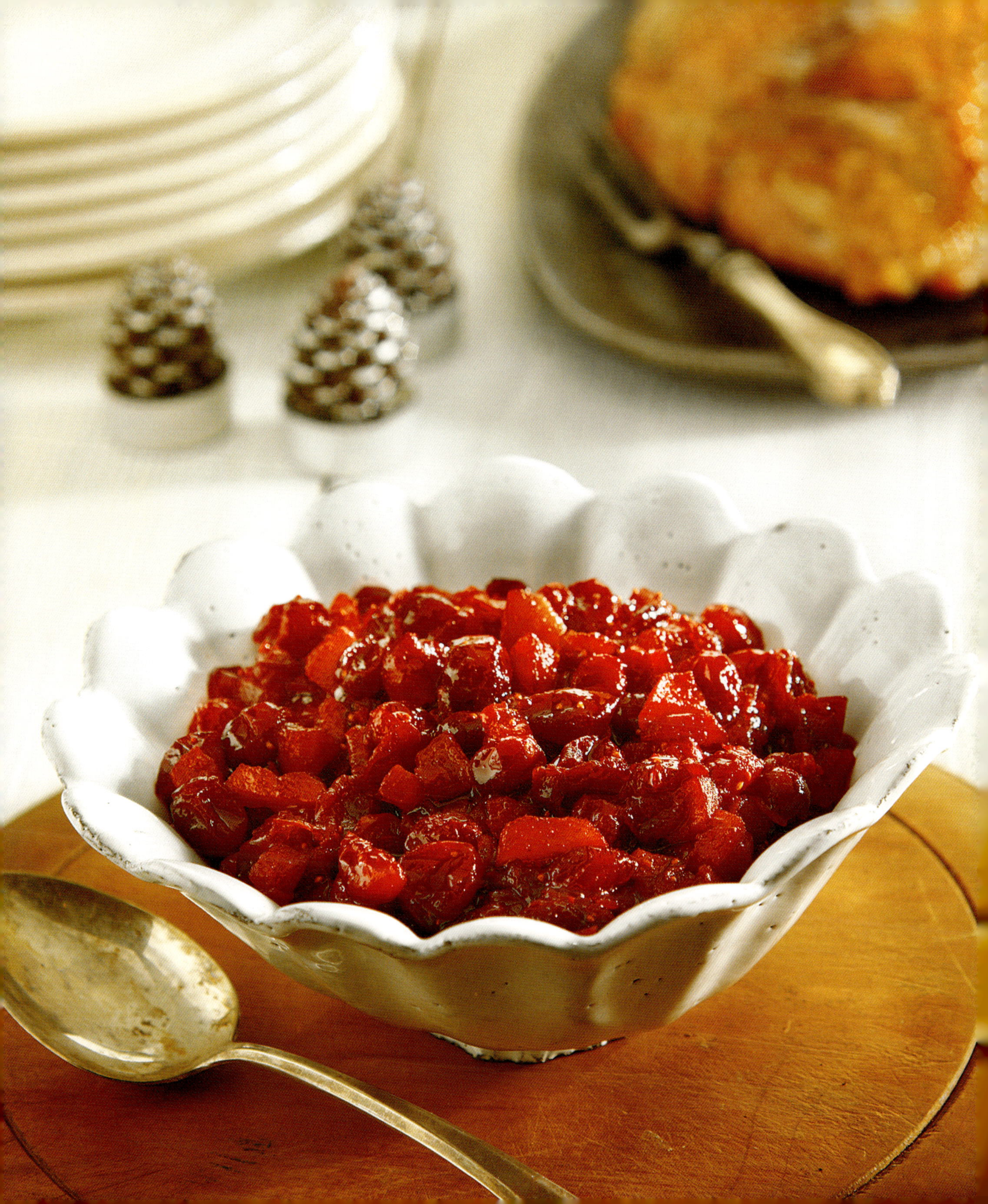

onion marmalade

Makes 5 cups

- 1 bottle (12 ounces) balsamic vinegar
- 1 bottle (12 ounces) white wine vinegar
- 3 tablespoons arrowroot or cornstarch
- 2 tablespoons water
- 1½ cups packed dark brown sugar
- 2 teaspoons cumin seeds
- 2 teaspoons coriander seeds
- 4 large yellow onions, halved and thinly sliced

Slow Cooker Directions

1. Cook vinegars in large saucepan over high heat until reduced to ¼ cup. Sauce will be thick and syrupy. Remove from heat. Blend arrowroot and water in small cup. Add brown sugar, cumin, coriander and arrowroot mixture to sauce; blend well.

2. Place onions in slow cooker. Stir in vinegar mixture; mix well. Cover; cook on LOW 8 to 10 hours or HIGH 4 to 6 hours or until onions are tender, stirring occasionally to prevent sticking. Store in refrigerator up to 2 weeks.

Serving Suggestion: Serve with eggs, roasted vegetables and meats, and on sandwiches.

honey citrus syrup

Makes 1 cup

- ½ cup honey
- ¼ cup lemon juice
- ¼ cup orange juice

Combine honey, lemon juice and orange juice in small bowl; stir until well blended. Refrigerate in airtight container until ready to use. Use syrup to sweeten tea and glaze fruits.

Favorite recipe from National Honey Board

onion marmalade

sweet freezer pickles

Makes about 6 cups

2 pounds cucumbers, unpeeled, sliced (about 4 medium)
1 medium red bell pepper, sliced
½ medium red onion, sliced
3 small carrots, quartered lengthwise, then cut into 3-inch pieces
1 medium celery stalk, finely chopped
¾ cup sugar
¾ cup cider vinegar
2 teaspoons mustard seeds *or* ¼ teaspoon red pepper flakes
1 teaspoon salt

1. Combine cucumbers, bell pepper, onion, carrots, celery, sugar, vinegar, mustard seeds and salt in large resealable food storage bag; mix well. Seal tightly, releasing excess air. Freeze at least 24 hours.

2. Remove from freezer; thaw at room temperature. Pour into large bowl; cover with plastic wrap. Refrigerate. (Flavors improve if thawed, then allowed to stand 2 days in refrigerator.) Store up to 3 weeks in refrigerator or 1 year in freezer.

honey chocolate sauce

Makes 2½ cups

1½ cups honey
1½ cups unsweetened cocoa
2 tablespoons butter or margarine

Microwave Directions
Combine honey, unsweetened cocoa and butter in small microwavable bowl; mix well. Cover with waxed paper and microwave at HIGH (100% power) 2 to 2½ minutes, stirring after 1 minute. Pour into sterilized gift jars. Keep refrigerated.

Favorite recipe from National Honey Board

sweet freezer pickles

horseradish sauce

Makes about 1¼ cups

  1 cup sour cream
¼ cup finely chopped fresh parsley
  1 tablespoon *each* prepared horseradish and Dijon mustard
½ teaspoon salt

Combine sour cream, parsley, horseradish, mustard and salt in small bowl until well blended. Store in airtight container in refrigerator up to 2 weeks.

twelve carat black-eyed pea relish

Makes 2 to 3 pints

12 small carrots, peeled
  1 cup white vinegar
¼ cup vegetable oil
  2 cans (about 15 ounces each) black-eyed peas, rinsed and drained
  1 sweet onion, chopped
  1 green bell pepper, finely chopped
  1 cup sugar
¼ cup Worcestershire sauce
    Salt and black pepper
    Dash ground red pepper

1. Place half of carrots in metal steamer or colander. Place steamer over a few inches of water in large saucepan with tight-fitting lid. Bring water to a boil; steam carrots 16 to 18 minutes or until crisp-tender, adding more water to saucepan, if necessary. Repeat with remaining carrots. Cool; coarsely chop carrots.

2. Combine vinegar and oil in small saucepan. Bring to a boil. Combine carrots, black-eyed peas, onion, bell pepper, sugar, Worcestershire sauce, salt, black pepper and ground red pepper in large bowl. Pour vinegar mixture over vegetable mixture.

3. Marinate, covered, in refrigerator at least 24 hours. Store, covered, in glass jars in refrigerator. Serve cold.

savory peanut butter dip

Makes 8 servings

¼ cup creamy peanut butter
3 ounces fat-free cream cheese
1 to 2 tablespoons lemon or apple juice
½ teaspoon ground cinnamon
⅛ to ¼ cup natural applesauce
2 apples, sliced
1 small banana, sliced
Celery stalks, sliced into 4-inch pieces
2 cups broccoli flowerets

Combine the peanut butter, cream cheese, juice and cinnamon in food processor. Blend until smooth. Add applesauce, little by little, to bring to the desired consistency for the dip. Chill before serving with fresh fruits or vegetables. Also try over baked sweet potatoes.

Favorite recipe from Peanut Advisory Board

spicy cocktail sauce

Makes 1⅓ cups

1 cup ketchup
2 cloves garlic, minced
1 tablespoon lemon juice
1 teaspoon prepared horseradish
¾ teaspoon chili powder
½ teaspoon salt
¼ teaspoon hot pepper sauce *or* ⅛ teaspoon ground red pepper

Combine ketchup, garlic, lemon juice, horseradish, chili powder, salt and hot pepper sauce in medium bowl; blend well. Spoon into glass bowl or jar; seal tightly. Store up to 1 month in refrigerator.

Note: Makes enough sauce for 1 pound of seafood.

spicy apple butter

Makes about 6 cups

5 pounds tart cooking apples (McIntosh, Granny Smith, Rome Beauty or York Imperial), peeled, cored and quartered (about 10 large apples)
1 cup sugar
½ cup apple juice
2 teaspoons ground cinnamon
½ teaspoon ground cloves
½ teaspoon ground allspice

Slow Cooker Directions

1. Combine all ingredients in slow cooker. Cover; cook on LOW 8 to 10 hours or until apples are very tender.

2. Mash apples with potato masher. Cook, uncovered, on LOW 2 hours or until thickened, stirring occasionally to prevent sticking.

Serving Suggestions: Homemade apple butter is a great alternative to store-bought jam or jelly on your favorite toast or muffin. For an instant dessert, try toasting a few slices of pound cake and spreading them with apple butter!

thick barbecue sauce

Makes 2 cups

2 medium onions, finely chopped
¾ cup cola
¾ cup ketchup
2 tablespoons white vinegar
2 tablespoons Worcestershire sauce
½ teaspoon chili powder
½ teaspoon salt

Combine all ingredients in medium saucepan over high heat. Bring to a boil. Cover; reduce heat and simmer about 45 minutes or until sauce is very thick, stirring occasionally.

173 - Classic Condiments

spicy apple butter

orange-zested dark cherry fruit relish

Makes 2⅔ cups

 1 package (1 pound) frozen unsweetened dark sweet cherries, partially thawed*
 ½ cup finely chopped red bell pepper
 ½ cup finely chopped green bell pepper
 ⅓ cup finely chopped red onion
 ½ cup raisins, dried cherries or dried cranberries
 1½ teaspoons grated orange peel
 2 tablespoons lemon juice
 ⅛ teaspoon red pepper flakes

Partially thawed cherries are easier to cut than thawed cherries.

Cut each cherry in half using serrated knife. Combine all ingredients in medium bowl; toss well. Let stand 15 minutes before serving.

Note: This makes a nice accompaniment to grilled pork or chicken.

cajun seasoning mix

Makes 1 cup

 ⅓ cup paprika (about 1 ounce)
 2 tablespoons garlic powder
 2 tablespoons onion powder
 1½ tablespoons ground red pepper
 1½ tablespoons dried oregano
 1½ tablespoons dried thyme
 1 tablespoon black pepper
 1 teaspoon dry mustard
 1 teaspoon sugar
 ½ teaspoon red pepper flakes

Whisk paprika, garlic powder, onion powder, ground red pepper, oregano, thyme, black pepper, dry mustard, sugar and red pepper flakes in small bowl. Store in airtight container.

175 - CLASSIC CONDIMENTS

orange-zested dark cherry fruit relish

honey strawberry preserves

Makes 3 pints

6 cups sliced strawberries
2 boxes (1¾ ounces each) powdered pectin
1¾ cups honey
2 tablespoons lemon juice

Combine strawberries and pectin in large saucepan; crush berries to blend completely. Bring mixture to a full rolling boil over medium-high heat. Boil hard 1 minute, stirring constantly. Stir in honey and lemon juice; return to a full rolling boil. Boil hard 5 minutes, stirring constantly. Remove from heat. Skim off foam. Ladle into clean, hot canning jars to within ¼ inch of tops. Seal according to manufacturer's directions. Place jars on rack in canner. Process 10 minutes in boiling water bath with boiling water 2 inches above jar tops. Remove jars from canner. Place on thick cloth or wire rack; cool away from drafts. After 12 hours test lids for proper seal; remove rings from sealed jars.

Favorite recipe from National Honey Board

creole dressing

Makes about 1 cup

¼ cup olive oil
2 tablespoons Creole or other whole grain mustard
2 tablespoons tomato juice
4 teaspoons red wine vinegar
1 teaspoon Worcestershire sauce
2 cloves garlic, minced
½ teaspoon dried thyme
¼ teaspoon ground red pepper

Combine oil, mustard, tomato juice, vinegar, Worcestershire sauce, garlic, thyme and red pepper in small bowl; whisk until blended. Store in airtight container in refrigerator up to 3 days.

clockwise from left: honey strawberry preserves, honey citrus syrup (page 166) and honey chocolate sauce (page 168)

quick refrigerator sweet pickles

Makes about 6 cups

5 cups thinly sliced cucumbers
2 cloves garlic, halved
2 cups water
1 teaspoon mustard seed
1 teaspoon celery seed
1 teaspoon ground turmeric
2 cups sliced onions
1 cup julienne carrots
2 cups vinegar
1½ cups EQUAL® SPOONFUL*

*May substitute 36 packets EQUAL® sweetener.

- Place cucumbers and garlic in glass bowl. Combine water, mustard seed, celery seed and turmeric in medium saucepan. Bring to boiling.

- Add onions and carrots; cook 2 minutes. Add vinegar; bring just to boiling.

- Remove from heat; stir in Equal®. Pour over cucumbers and garlic. Cool.

- Cover and chill at least 24 hours before serving. Store in refrigerator up to 2 weeks.

spiced peach sauce

Makes about 3 cups

2 packages (16 ounces each) frozen unsweetened sliced peaches, thawed
2 cups sugar
1½ teaspoons lemon juice
1½ teaspoons ground cinnamon
¼ teaspoon ground nutmeg

1. Combine peaches and thawing liquid, sugar, lemon juice, cinnamon and nutmeg in heavy medium saucepan; bring to a boil over high heat. Boil 45 to 50 minutes or until thickened, stirring occasionally and breaking peaches into small pieces with back of wooden spoon.

2. Remove saucepan from heat; cool completely. Store in airtight container in refrigerator up to 2 months.

Serving Suggestion: Serve with waffles or pancakes.

texas hot & tangy bbq sauce

Makes 5¼ cups

¼ cup vegetable oil
2 cups finely chopped onions
6 cloves garlic, minced
2 cups water
1 can (12 ounces) tomato paste
1 cup packed brown sugar
¾ cup cider vinegar
½ cup molasses
¼ cup Worcestershire sauce
2 tablespoons hot pepper sauce
2 teaspoons chili powder
2 teaspoons ground cumin
½ teaspoon ground red pepper

1. Heat oil in large skillet over medium-high heat. Add onions; cook and stir 8 to 10 minutes or until onions begin to brown. Add garlic; cook 2 minutes. Add water, tomato paste, brown sugar, vinegar, molasses, Worcestershire sauce, hot pepper sauce, chili powder, cumin and red pepper; whisk until well blended.

2. Reduce heat to medium-low; simmer 15 minutes, stirring occasionally. Cover and remove from heat. Cool 30 minutes. Store in refrigerator up to 3 weeks.

gingered apple-cranberry chutney

Makes about 6 servings

2 medium Granny Smith apples, peeled and diced
1 package (12 ounces) fresh or thawed frozen cranberries
1¼ cups packed light brown sugar
¾ cup cranberry juice cocktail
½ cup golden raisins
¼ cup chopped crystallized ginger
¼ cup cider vinegar
1 teaspoon ground cinnamon
⅛ teaspoon ground allspice

1. Combine apples, cranberries, brown sugar, juice cocktail, raisins, ginger, vinegar, cinnamon and allspice in heavy medium saucepan; bring to a boil over high heat. Reduce heat to medium. Simmer 20 to 25 minutes or until mixture is very thick, stirring occasionally.

2. Remove saucepan from heat. Cool completely. Store in airtight container in refrigerator up to 2 weeks.

honey brandy spread

Makes 1 cup

2 tablespoons butter or margarine, softened
¾ cup creamed honey
1 tablespoon brandy*
Dash ground nutmeg

1 teaspoon brandy flavoring can be substituted for brandy.

Beat butter in small bowl until creamy. Gradually stir in honey; beat until smooth. Stir in brandy and nutmeg. Refrigerate until ready to serve. Use as a spread on quick breads or dollop on grilled chicken.

Favorite recipe from National Honey Board

181 - Classic Condiments

gingered apple-cranberry chutney

refrigerator corn relish

Makes 10 servings

- 2 cups cut fresh corn (4 ears) *or* 1 (10-ounce) package frozen whole-kernel corn
- ½ cup vinegar
- ⅓ cup cold water
- 1 tablespoon cornstarch
- ¼ cup chopped onion
- ¼ cup chopped celery
- ¼ cup chopped green or red bell pepper
- 2 tablespoons chopped pimiento
- 1 teaspoon ground turmeric
- ½ teaspoon salt
- ½ teaspoon dry mustard
- ¼ cup EQUAL® SPOONFUL*

*May substitute 6 packets EQUAL® sweetener.

- Cook corn in boiling water until crisp-tender, 5 to 7 minutes; drain and set aside.

- Combine vinegar, water and cornstarch in large saucepan; stir until cornstarch is dissolved. Add corn, onion, celery, pepper, pimiento, turmeric, salt and mustard. Cook and stir until thickened and bubbly. Cook and stir 2 minutes more. Remove from heat; stir in Equal®. Cool. Cover and store in refrigerator up to 2 weeks.

- Serve with beef, pork or poultry.

183 - Classic Condiments

left to right: refrigerator corn relish and quick refrigerator sweet pickles (page 178)

cran-apple orange conserve

Makes about 5 cups

    2 medium oranges
    5 large tart apples, peeled, cored and chopped
    2 cups sugar
1½ cups fresh cranberries
    1 tablespoon grated lemon peel
      Pound cake

Slow Cooker Directions

1. Remove thin slice from both ends of each orange for easier chopping. Finely chop unpeeled oranges to make 2 cups; remove any seeds. Combine oranges, apples, sugar, cranberries and lemon peel in slow cooker. Cover; cook on HIGH 4 hours.

2. Slightly crush fruit with potato masher. *Turn temperature to LOW.* Cook, uncovered, on LOW 4 hours or until very thick, stirring occasionally to prevent sticking. Cool at least 2 hours. Serve with pound cake.

Serving Suggestion: Fruit conserve can also be served with roast pork or poultry.

185 - CLASSIC CONDIMENTS

cran-apple orange conserve

The publisher would like to thank the companies and organizations listed below for the use of their recipes and photographs in this publication.

Cabot® Creamery Cooperative

Campbell Soup Company

Chef Paul Prudhomme's Magic Seasoning Blends®

Cream of Wheat® Cereal

Del Monte Foods

Dole Food Company, Inc.

Duncan Hines® and Moist Deluxe® are registered trademarks of Pinnacle Foods Corp.

Equal® sweetener

McIlhenny Company (TABASCO® brand Pepper Sauce)

National Honey Board

Ortega®, A Division of B&G Foods, Inc.

Peanut Advisory Board

The Quaker® Oatmeal Kitchens

Reckitt Benckiser LLC.

Riviana Foods Inc.

Reprinted with permission of Sunkist Growers, Inc. All Rights Reserved.

Unilever

A

Almonds: Fresh Berry-Berry Cobbler, 156
Ambrosia, 158
Apple
  Cran-Apple Orange Conserve, 184
  Cranberry-Apple Chutney, 164
  Gingered Apple-Cranberry Chutney, 180
  Savory Peanut Butter Dip, 171
  Southern Caramel Apple Bars, 146
  Spicy Apple Butter, 172
  Sweet Potato & Pecan Casserole, 122
Apricot Coleslaw, 120

B

Bacon
  Bacon-Cheese Grits, 110
  Black-Eyed Pea Soup, 44
  Brandy-Soaked Scallops, 4
  Country-Style Corn, 110
  Thick and Creamy Succotash Soup, 48
Bacon-Cheese Grits, 110
Baked Beer-Battered Onions and Shrimp, 14
Baked Halibut Creole, 100
Banana Praline Ice Cream Cake, 126
Bananas
  Ambrosia, 158
  Banana Praline Ice Cream Cake, 126
  Savory Peanut Butter Dip, 171
  Sweet and Spicy Bananas Foster, 159
  Tropical Bananas Foster Upside-Down Cake, 142
Barbecue Ranch Chicken Salad, 115
Barley and Sausage Gumbo, 56
Bayou Dirty Rice, 112
Bayou Yam Muffins, 30
BBQ Short Ribs with Cola Sauce, 71
Beans, Black: Barbecue Ranch Chicken Salad, 115
Beans, Kidney
  Cajun-Style Beef and Beans, 74
  Ham & Barbecued Bean Skillet, 82
  Red Bean Soup with Andouille Sausage, 58
Beans, Lima
  New Orleans Pork Gumbo, 59
  Southern-Style Succotash, 120
  Thick and Creamy Succotash Soup, 48
Beans, Red
  Creole Red Bean and Rice Salad, 116
  Red Beans & Rice, 122
Beef
  BBQ Short Ribs with Cola Sauce, 71
  Cajun-Style Beef and Beans, 74
  Smoky Barbecued Beef Sandwiches, 78
Benne Wafers, 160
Berry
  Cran-Apple Orange Conserve, 184
  Cranberry-Apple Chutney, 164
  Fresh Berry-Berry Cobbler, 156
  Gingered Apple-Cranberry Chutney, 180
  Honey Strawberry Preserves, 176
  Hot Pepper Cranberry Jelly Appetizer, 8
  Pulled Pork Sandwiches, 70
  Strawberry Shortcake, 162

Beverages
  Lemon Herbal Iced Tea, 16
  Orange Iced Tea, 23
  Pineapple-Mint Lemonade, 18
  Summer Spritzer, 18
Biscuits
  Cheese-Topped Ham Biscuits, 24
  Green Onion Cream Cheese Breakfast Biscuits, 36
  Honey Sweet Potato Biscuits, 28
  Sawmill Biscuits and Gravy, 32
  Southern Country Chicken and Biscuits, 72
  Strawberry Shortcake, 162
Black Bottom Pie, 136
Blackened Catfish with Easy Tartar Sauce and Rice, 102
Black-Eyed Pea and Chicken Salad, 106
Black-Eyed Peas
  Black-Eyed Pea and Chicken Salad, 106
  Black-Eyed Pea Soup, 44
  Corn and Black-Eyed Pea Salad, 123
  Hoppin' John, 68
  Hoppin' Shrimp and Brown Rice, 94
  Twelve Carat Black-Eyed Pea Relish, 170
Black-Eyed Pea Soup, 44
Brandy-Soaked Scallops, 4
Broiled Cajun Fish Fillets, 88

C

Cajun Blackened Tuna, 92
Cajun Dirty Rice, 109
Cajun Sausage and Rice, 80
Cajun Seasoning, 74
Cajun Seasoning Mix, 174
Cajun-Style Beef and Beans, 74
Cajun-Style Chicken Soup, 60

Caramel
  Banana Praline Ice Cream Cake, 126
  Pecan Bread Pudding with Caramel Whiskey Sauce, 154
  Southern Caramel Apple Bars, 146
  Turtle Pecan Pie, 131

Carolina-Style Barbecue Chicken, 76
Carrot Raisin Salad, 112
Charleston Crab Soup, 54
Cheddar-Beer Hush Puppies, 10
Cheese-Topped Ham Biscuits, 24
Chicken & Sausage Gumbo, 46
Chicken Étouffé with Pasta, 77

Chocolate
  Banana Praline Ice Cream Cake, 126
  Black Bottom Pie, 136
  Chocolate Chess Pie, 134
  Extra Chunky Peanut Butter Cookies, 158
  Fudge Rum Balls, 151
  Honey Chocolate Sauce, 168
  Mississippi Mud Bars, 152
  Turtle Pecan Pie, 131

Chocolate Chess Pie, 134

Coconut
  Ambrosia, 158
  Sweet Coconut Custard Pie, 137
  Tropical Bananas Foster Upside-Down Cake, 142

Cookies and Bars
  Benne Wafers, 160
  Extra Chunky Peanut Butter Cookies, 158
  Mississippi Mud Bars, 152
  Southern Caramel Apple Bars, 146

Corn
  Barbecue Ranch Chicken Salad, 115
  Corn and Black-Eyed Pea Salad, 123
  Corn Fritters, 6
  Country-Style Corn, 110
  Grilled Corn on the Cob with Buttery Citrus Spread, 118
  New Orleans Pork Gumbo, 59
  Refrigerator Corn Relish, 182
  Savory Corn Cakes, 26
  Southern Pecan Cornbread Stuffing, 114
  Southern-Style Succotash, 120
  Thick and Creamy Succotash Soup, 48
  Tomato Chicken Gumbo, 53

Corn and Black-Eyed Pea Salad, 123
Corn Fritters, 6
Country-Style Corn, 110
Crab Canapés, 16
Cran-Apple Orange Conserve, 184
Cranberry-Apple Chutney, 164
Creole Dressing, 176
Creole Red Bean and Rice Salad, 116

D
Dinner Rolls, 38
Dips and Spreads
  Honey Brandy Spread, 180
  Hot Crab-Cheddar Spread, 8
  Savory Peanut Butter Dip, 171
  Southern Pimiento Cheese, 13

E
Easy Tartar Sauce, 102
Extra Chunky Peanut Butter Cookies, 158

F
Fish and Seafood (pages 84-103)
  Baked Beer-Battered Onions and Shrimp, 14
  Brandy-Soaked Scallops, 4
  Charleston Crab Soup, 54
  Crab Canapés, 16
  Hot Crab-Cheddar Spread, 8
  Louisiana Gumbo, 50
  Shrimp Toast, 12
  Spicy Shrimp Gumbo, 62
  Zesty Crab Cakes with Red Pepper Sauce, 22

Fresh Berry-Berry Cobbler, 156
Fried Green Tomatoes, 20
Fudge Rum Balls, 151

G
Garlicky Mustard Greens, 114
Gingered Apple-Cranberry Chutney, 180
Glazed Maple Acorn Squash, 118
Green Onion Cream Cheese Breakfast Biscuits, 36
Grilled Cajun Potato Wedges, 108
Grilled Corn on the Cob with Buttery Citrus Spread, 118
Grilled Muffuletta, 68

Grits
  Bacon-Cheese Grits, 110
  Shrimp and Garlic-Parmesan Grits, 98

H
Ham
  Black-Eyed Pea Soup, 44
  Cheese-Topped Ham Biscuits, 24
  Grilled Muffuletta, 68

Ham *(continued)*
    Ham & Barbecued Bean Skillet, 82
    Red Bean Soup with Andouille Sausage, 58
    Shrimp Toast, 12
Ham & Barbecued Bean Skillet, 82
Honey
    BBQ Short Ribs with Cola Sauce, 71
    Honey Brandy Spread, 180
    Honey Chocolate Sauce, 168
    Honey Citrus Syrup, 166
    Honey Strawberry Preserves, 176
    Honey Sweet Potato Biscuits, 28
Honey Brandy Spread, 180
Honey Chocolate Sauce, 168
Honey Citrus Syrup, 166
Honey Strawberry Preserves, 176
Honey Sweet Potato Biscuits, 28
Hoppin' John, 68
Hoppin' Shrimp and Brown Rice, 94
Horseradish Sauce, 170
Hot Crab-Cheddar Spread, 8
Hot Pepper Cranberry Jelly Appetizer, 8
Hush Puppies, 104
Hush Puppies
    Cheddar-Beer Hush Puppies, 10
    Hush Puppies, 96
    Southern Fried Catfish with Hush Puppies, 96

J
Jam, Jelly and Marmalade
    Cran-Apple Orange Conserve, 184
    Honey Strawberry Preserves, 176

Jam, Jelly and Marmalade *(continued)*
    Hot Pepper Cranberry Jelly Appetizer, 8
    Onion Marmalade, 166
Jambalaya, 86

L
Lemon
    Honey Citrus Syrup, 166
    Lemon Chess Pie, 140
    Lemon Herbal Iced Tea, 16
    Pineapple-Mint Lemonade, 18
    Summer Spritzer, 18
Lemon Chess Pie, 140
Lemon Herbal Iced Tea, 16
Louisiana Gumbo, 50

M
Magic Fried Oysters, 100
Microwave Recipes: Honey Chocolate Sauce, 168
Mini Corn Bread Muffins, 34
Mississippi Mud Bars, 152
Muffins
    Bayou Yam Muffins, 30
    Mini Corn Bread Muffins, 34

N
New Orleans Pork Gumbo, 59

O
Oaty Pear 'n' Pecan Pancakes, 40
Okra
    Barley and Sausage Gumbo, 56
    Cajun-Style Chicken Soup, 60
    Hoppin' Shrimp and Brown Rice, 94
    Louisiana Gumbo, 50
    New Orleans Pork Gumbo, 59
    Spicy Shrimp Gumbo, 62

Onion Marmalade, 166
Orange
    Ambrosia, 158
    Cran-Apple Orange Conserve, 184
    Honey Citrus Syrup, 166
    Orange Iced Tea, 23
    Orange-Zested Dark Cherry Fruit Relish, 174
    Southern Pecan Cornbread Stuffing, 114
    Strawberry Shortcake, 162
    Sweet Potato Crumb Cake, 138
Orange Iced Tea, 23
Orange-Zested Dark Cherry Fruit Relish, 174
Oyster Po' Boys, 91

P
Peach Cobbler, 150
Peaches
    Peach Cobbler, 150
    Peach Turnovers, 144
    Spiced Peach Sauce, 178
Peach Turnovers, 144
Peanut Butter
    Extra Chunky Peanut Butter Cookies, 158
    Savory Peanut Butter Dip, 171
    Southern Peanut Butter Cheesecake, 150
Peanuts: Extra Chunky Peanut Butter Cookies, 158
Pecan Bread Pudding with Caramel Whiskey Sauce, 154
Pecan Praline Brandy Cake, 132
Pecans
    Banana Praline Ice Cream Cake, 126
    Fudge Rum Balls, 151
    Oaty Pear 'n' Pecan Pancakes, 40

Pecans *(continued)*
   Pecan Bread Pudding with Caramel Whiskey Sauce, 154
   Pecan Praline Brandy Cake, 132
   Southern Caramel Apple Bars, 146
   Southern Pecan Cornbread Stuffing, 114
   Sweet Potato & Pecan Casserole, 122
   Sweet Potato Crumb Cake, 138
   Turtle Pecan Pie, 131

Pickles
   Quick Refrigerator Sweet Pickles, 178
   Sweet Freezer Pickles, 168

Pineapple-Mint Lemonade, 18

Pork *(see also* **Bacon, Ham** *and* **Sausage***)*
   New Orleans Pork Gumbo, 59
   Pork and Corn Bread Stuffing Casserole, 66
   Pulled Pork Sandwiches, 70

Pork and Corn Bread Stuffing Casserole, 66

Potatoes *(see also* **Potatoes, Sweet***)*
   Black-Eyed Pea Soup, 44
   Grilled Cajun Potato Wedges, 108
   Southern Country Chicken and Biscuits, 72

Potatoes, Sweet
   Bayou Yam Muffins, 30
   Honey Sweet Potato Biscuits, 28
   Red Bean Soup with Andouille Sausage, 58
   Steamed Southern Sweet Potato Custard, 148

Potatoes, Sweet *(continued)*
   Sweet Potato & Pecan Casserole, 122
   Sweet Potato Crumb Cake, 138
   Sweet Potato Fries, 18
   Sweet Potato Pie, 130

Poultry
   Barbecue Ranch Chicken Salad, 115
   Barley and Sausage Gumbo, 56
   Black-Eyed Pea and Chicken Salad, 106
   Cajun-Style Chicken Soup, 60
   Carolina-Style Barbecue Chicken, 76
   Chicken & Sausage Gumbo, 46
   Chicken Étouffé with Pasta, 77
   Hoppin' John, 68
   Louisiana Gumbo, 50
   Southern Country Chicken and Biscuits, 72
   Spicy Buttermilk Oven-Fried Chicken, 64
   Tomato Chicken Gumbo, 53

Pulled Pork Sandwiches, 70

Q
Quick Refrigerator Sweet Pickles, 178

R
Red Beans & Rice, 122
Red Bean Soup with Andouille Sausage, 58
Red Pepper Sauce, 23
Refrigerator Corn Relish, 182

Relish and Chutney
   Cranberry-Apple Chutney, 164
   Gingered Apple-Cranberry Chutney, 180

Relish and Chutney *(continued)*
   Orange-Zested Dark Cherry Fruit Relish, 174
   Refrigerator Corn Relish, 182
   Twelve Carat Black-Eyed Pea Relish, 170

Rice
   Bayou Dirty Rice, 112
   Blackened Catfish with Easy Tartar Sauce and Rice, 102
   Cajun Dirty Rice, 109
   Cajun Sausage and Rice, 80
   Cajun-Style Beef and Beans, 74
   Cajun-Style Chicken Soup, 60
   Creole Red Bean and Rice Salad, 116
   Hoppin' John, 68
   Hoppin' Shrimp and Brown Rice, 94
   Jambalaya, 86
   Louisiana Gumbo, 50
   Red Beans & Rice, 122
   Shrimp Creole, 90
   Spicy Shrimp Gumbo, 62
   Tomato Chicken Gumbo, 53

S
Sandwiches
   Grilled Muffuletta, 68
   Oyster Po' Boys, 91
   Pulled Pork Sandwiches, 70
   Smoky Barbecued Beef Sandwiches, 78

Sauces
   Blackened Catfish with Easy Tartar Sauce and Rice, 102
   Easy Tartar Sauce, 102
   Honey Chocolate Sauce, 168
   Horseradish Sauce, 170
   Red Pepper Sauce, 23
   Spiced Peach Sauce, 178
   Spicy Cocktail Sauce, 171

Sauces *(continued)*
   Texas Hot & Tangy BBQ Sauce, 179
   Thick Barbecue Sauce, 172

Sausage
   Barley and Sausage Gumbo, 56
   Bayou Dirty Rice, 112
   Cajun Dirty Rice, 109
   Cajun Sausage and Rice, 80
   Chicken & Sausage Gumbo, 46
   Hoppin' John, 68
   Jambalaya, 86
   Louisiana Gumbo, 50
   Red Bean Soup with Andouille Sausage, 58
   Sausage and Cheddar Corn Bread, 42
   Sawmill Biscuits and Gravy, 32
   Tomato Chicken Gumbo, 53

Sausage and Cheddar Corn Bread, 42
Savory Corn Cakes, 26
Savory Peanut Butter Dip, 171
Sawmill Biscuits and Gravy, 32
Shoo Fly Pie, 128
Shrimp and Garlic-Parmesan Grits, 98
Shrimp Creole, 90
Shrimp Toast, 12

Slow Cooker Recipes
   Barley and Sausage Gumbo, 56
   Cajun Sausage and Rice, 80
   Cran-Apple Orange Conserve, 184
   Onion Marmalade, 166
   Peach Cobbler, 150
   Red Beans & Rice, 122
   Red Bean Soup with Andouille Sausage, 58
   Spicy Apple Butter, 172
   Spinach Spoon Bread, 31

Slow Cooker Recipes *(continued)*
   Steamed Southern Sweet Potato Custard, 148
   Sweet Potato & Pecan Casserole, 122

Smoky Barbecued Beef Sandwiches, 78
Southern Caramel Apple Bars, 146
Southern Country Chicken and Biscuits, 72
Southern Crab Cakes with Rémoulade Dipping Sauce, 84
Southern Fried Catfish with Hush Puppies, 96
Southern Oatmeal Pie, 124
Southern Peanut Butter Cheesecake, 150
Southern Pecan Cornbread Stuffing, 114
Southern Pimiento Cheese, 13
Southern Spoon Bread, 39
Southern-Style Succotash, 120
Spiced Peach Sauce, 178
Spicy Apple Butter, 172
Spicy Buttermilk Oven-Fried Chicken, 64
Spicy Cocktail Sauce, 171
Spicy Mayonnaise, 91
Spicy Pumpkin Soup with Green Chile Swirl, 52
Spicy Shrimp Gumbo, 62
Spinach Spoon Bread, 31
Steamed Southern Sweet Potato Custard, 148
Strawberry Shortcake, 162
Summer Spritzer, 18
Sweet and Spicy Bananas Foster, 159
Sweet Coconut Custard Pie, 137
Sweet Freezer Pickles, 168
Sweet Potato & Pecan Casserole, 122
Sweet Potato Crumb Cake, 138

Sweet Potato Fries, 18
Sweet Potato Pie, 130

T
Texas Hot & Tangy BBQ Sauce, 179
Thick and Creamy Succotash Soup, 48
Thick Barbecue Sauce, 172
Tomato Chicken Gumbo, 53
Tropical Bananas Foster Upside-Down Cake, 142
Turtle Pecan Pie, 131
Twelve Carat Black-Eyed Pea Relish, 170

W
Walnuts: Mississippi Mud Bars, 152

Z
Zesty Crab Cakes with Red Pepper Sauce, 22

VOLUME MEASUREMENTS (dry)

1/8 teaspoon = 0.5 mL
1/4 teaspoon = 1 mL
1/2 teaspoon = 2 mL
3/4 teaspoon = 4 mL
1 teaspoon = 5 mL
1 tablespoon = 15 mL
2 tablespoons = 30 mL
1/4 cup = 60 mL
1/3 cup = 75 mL
1/2 cup = 125 mL
2/3 cup = 150 mL
3/4 cup = 175 mL
1 cup = 250 mL
2 cups = 1 pint = 500 mL
3 cups = 750 mL
4 cups = 1 quart = 1 L

VOLUME MEASUREMENTS (fluid)

1 fluid ounce (2 tablespoons) = 30 mL
4 fluid ounces (1/2 cup) = 125 mL
8 fluid ounces (1 cup) = 250 mL
12 fluid ounces (1 1/2 cups) = 375 mL
16 fluid ounces (2 cups) = 500 mL

WEIGHTS (mass)

1/2 ounce = 15 g
1 ounce = 30 g
3 ounces = 90 g
4 ounces = 120 g
8 ounces = 225 g
10 ounces = 285 g
12 ounces = 360 g
16 ounces = 1 pound = 450 g

DIMENSIONS

1/16 inch = 2 mm
1/8 inch = 3 mm
1/4 inch = 6 mm
1/2 inch = 1.5 cm
3/4 inch = 2 cm
1 inch = 2.5 cm

OVEN TEMPERATURES

250°F = 120°C
275°F = 140°C
300°F = 150°C
325°F = 160°C
350°F = 180°C
375°F = 190°C
400°F = 200°C
425°F = 220°C
450°F = 230°C

BAKING PAN SIZES

Utensil	Size in Inches/Quarts	Metric Volume	Size in Centimeters
Baking or Cake Pan (square or rectangular)	8×8×2	2 L	20×20×5
	9×9×2	2.5 L	23×23×5
	12×8×2	3 L	30×20×5
	13×9×2	3.5 L	33×23×5
Loaf Pan	8×4×3	1.5 L	20×10×7
	9×5×3	2 L	23×13×7
Round Layer Cake Pan	8×1 1/2	1.2 L	20×4
	9×1 1/2	1.5 L	23×4
Pie Plate	8×1 1/4	750 mL	20×3
	9×1 1/4	1 L	23×3
Baking Dish or Casserole	1 quart	1 L	—
	1 1/2 quart	1.5 L	—
	2 quart	2 L	—